Ensemble Deep Learning for Traffic Flow Prediction and Intelligent Transportation Modeling

Author: Nilofour

Table of Contents

Chapter 1: Introduction

In recent decades, rapid urbanisation and increasing motorisation have raised growing concerns regarding urban traffic congestion, especially in developing countries. As it now seems trite to say, traffic congestion is a serious challenge, not just because of the social costs associated with travel time and fuel consumed while idling, but also because of the wider implications for public health, and associated economic productivity, sustainability, and the environment. With increasing numbers of vehicles on the streets, outdated road infrastructure, and uncoordinated and fragmented traffic management organisations, a comprehensive solution to urban congestion requires the development of advanced, intelligent, data-driven solutions to identify and manage urban congestion.

Traffic congestion in urban areas is one of the biggest problems confronting many modern cities today, especially those in developing nations. With population growth, urban sprawl, and vehicle ownership increasing dramatically, the cities are experiencing gridlock, longer commutes, and increased pollution. Compounding these issues are poor road infrastructure, often manual traffic management systems, and a complete lack of real-time traffic management systems in many cities (Shanmugam, A. et al., 2024) Conventional traffic forecasting techniques are defined by fixed rules or statistical models and do not account for the always-changing, dynamic, and context-specific nature of traffic flow, where there are high variability levels in road usage. In addition, such models do not incorporate a plethora of influencing factors, including weather conditions (precipitation), time of day, road incidents, or surges due to social or political events. While intelligent traffic management systems (ITMS) have begun to deploy in some metro cities are often limited, non-standardised, and underutilise real-time data and sources of analytics. Moreover, there is a significant gap in applying deep learning and ensemble deep learning approaches leveraging Bengaluru traffic data (real traffic data) to produce more reliable and valid congestion prediction models.

The developments in intelligent transportation systems (ITS) have profited well from introducing artificial intelligence, deep learning, and computer vision technologies (Manguri et al., 2023). Researchers and policymakers are increasingly relying on these technologies to enable means and ways to monitor traffic flow and estimate demand for those road infrastructures (Luo, X et al., 2019). This research presents a study on developing an ensemble deep learning framework to predict urban traffic congestion by aligning multimodal data from video analytics and meteorological conditions. The remainder of this chapter explicates the background, motivation, objectives, and scope of the research (Lin et al., 2018).

Intelligent Transport Systems (ITS) are a necessity in today's transport systems and offer considerable potential for research and development. Frameworks for intelligent transportation systems were directed by the USDOT ITS documentation (United States Department of Transportation, n.d.). To illustrate, the ITS market in the Middle East was worth USD 2.82 billion in 2017 and is looking to sustain a steady compound annual growth rate (CAGR) of 11.6% over the forecast period. One particular trend driving growth in this market is the growing demand for real-time updates on traffic issues for drivers and passengers. ITS offers a way to address the increasing difficulties of traffic congestion and also addresses the issues of safety and efficiency in transportation systems. ITS includes many things, many sensors, combinations of networks, data, and a collection of things in a real-time environment to help collect data, enrich intelligence, and operate traffic. However, a growing number of vehicles using our roads has created many challenges, such as traffic congestion, collisions, delays to the movement of people and goods, and environmental concerns.

The traffic volume component in the ITS environment continues to grow, and as the number of vehicles continues to increase, traffic conditions will continue to exceed the traffic-control capability of urban infrastructure and management, which will only see increasing amounts of traffic jams and deteriorating road safety (Najjar et al., 2017). More specifically, delay and congestion generally occur at intersections. (Coello et al. 2024) ITS takes many actions to reduce and relieve congestion. Some minor components include the collection of traffic flow data, which can cause changes in traffic signals and possibly reduce congestion for considerable periods. Congestion pricing, as implemented or as tolls or required fees, induces high-occupancy vehicles (and the reduction of single-occupants) onto some streets and helps make public transport and shared transport more accessible and affordable.

ITS, in addition to helping to reduce congestion, includes encouraging alternative and non-motorised travel modes to improve road safety for vehicles and pedestrians (Sim, K., et al, 2022). These initiatives will result in an automatic traffic rules enforcement device and lead to fines for the misuse of traffic rules, such as running red lights or speeding. With continuous monitoring during driving time, ITS will encourage compliance with traffic rules (and subsequently, reduce accidents). (Huang et al., 2022) Intelligent infrastructure is another applicable concept in ITS to improve road safety support. Connected pedestrian crossings and dedicated on-road space for emergency vehicles improve accident reduction for those who need it. Acknowledging the important role of an ITS, presented with a unique chance to change transportation systems regarding data-driven decisions and new technologies. (Khalil et al. 2024) The basic principle of including Deep Learning (DL) models into ITS allows us to unleash the hidden possibilities of complex transportation data. This allows us to accurately predict traffic situations, recognise and classify objects, and create innovative, smart plans of action for a smooth and excellent travel experience.

The complexity of IT is part of the need for a robust algorithm that computes with big data (that is, big data isn't just for the sake of it, it's a class of research where data size scales) and appropriate algorithms. Machine Learning (ML) gives a wide range of algorithms for various tasks: classification, regression, ranking, clustering, and dimensionality reduction (Song, W. et al., 2022). These ML algorithms can be 'trained' in several learning situations: supervised, unsupervised, semi-supervised, online, reinforcement, active learning, and in federated learning (FL). DL is a subset of ML and has particular potential within ITS (Cella, 2023). DL models have no limits in handling large and diverse data (covering a range of variables in transportation), which may include vehicle characteristics, road conditions, traffic flows, passenger behaviours, etc.

DL allows a system to identify, detect, recognise, and predict many variables needed to properly evaluate and manage ITS. In the context of ITS, DL shows value by being able to process and assess different data points from various possible channels: e.g., traffic cameras, sensors, historical transport data, etc. This gives a broader opportunity for innovative solutions for traffic forecasting, congestion diversion, or routing. Of course, some DL models (e.g., CNN, LSTM, etc.) have demonstrated a particular promise in detection, prediction, classification tasks (e.g., vehicles, traffic signs, etc.) or prediction of driver behaviour, etc., a smart vision-based system that, using fisheye cameras and self-learning algorithms, counts vehicles coming to and from intersections precisely. (Adl et al., 2024) This method (and solution) is designed to be scalable and low-cost for many implementations, while improving the monitoring of traffic flows. And Cella (2023) proposes a hybrid neural network system that utilises social data sources to improve rider satisfaction with intelligent transportation systems. The patented approach optimises transportation services through user-oriented data combination methods and predictive models.

DL plays a multi-faceted role in changing traditional ITS, such as flow predictions, incident detection, vehicle detection and classification, traffic sign recognition, autonomous driving, and more (Lee & Kim, 2018; Kuutti et al., 2021). Recently, DL has been identified as a specific and promising method of managing complex challenges with ITS. DL-based ITS systems utilise many technologies, including artificial intelligence, to realise improvements in efficiency, safety, and mobility, utilising intelligent information and communication technologies. (Wan et al., 2021) DL algorithms have a distinct adaptability, allowing them to learn from a highly diverse group of datasets, extract complex patterns, and make accurate predictions, allowing algorithms to be optimised. Since DL is best suited to addressing challenges internally, with challenges in ITS (Verma et al. 2025).

Traffic flow prediction is one of the major applications of DL in ITS. Advanced DL algorithms can analyse and understand massive amounts of historic and real-time traffic data to notice complex relationships and patterns when analysing aggregate data for the flow of traffic. DL models can reliably make short-term predictions about future traffic conditions based on volume, speed, and density of the road network. Improved accuracy of traffic flow predictions allows transportation authorities to better manage traffic flow through signal timing optimisation, ramp metering changes, or congestion-aware route guidance. Improved short-term traffic modelling of traffic flow allows for proactive congestion mitigation and improves overall network efficiency. Moreover, to accurately model the short-term traffic, improved short-term traffic modelling through DL allows authorities to optimise traffic management through adaptation, or the guidance of congestion-aware strategies permits congestion avoidance as well as improves overall traffic efficiency. While these AI-enabled predictive capacities might not change the emphasis cities will place on key performance indicators (KPI) of traffic, transit agencies may be able to take advantage of them and improve both their relationship with the traffic department relative to their delay targets in traffic management, as well as the intelligent urban and regional transportation systems (Jeon et al., 2018).

Vehicle classification is one of the most important examples of applying DL. It is equally the most important ITS application utilising DL video analytics (Wan et al., 2021). DNNs can be trained on image datasets including a variety of different types of vehicles, including cars, trucks, buses, motorcycles, etc. Utilising DL models for vehicle classification can be effectively relied upon to identify and classify vehicles in real-time, by processing a live video stream of traffic using traffic cameras. Accurate vehicle classification allows for intelligent tolling systems to charge different vehicles correctly (Sim, K., et al, 2022). It also allows transportation agencies to obtain traffic metrics that are associated with each type of vehicle, and can help monitor and analyse overall road usage patterns. (Yu et al., 2021) By using DL analyses of visible vehicle data for vehicle classification, transportation officials can have a greater situational awareness of their networks and develop more targeted (and thereby more efficient) transportation management strategies for urban and rural road networks.

Incident detection is a key use of DL in ITS by constantly analysing live video traffic feeds from traffic cameras located throughout urban cities. DNNs can autonomously detect a variety of traffic incidents, including crashes, disabled vehicles, or debris on the roadway. (Pathik et al., 2022; Bhuvaneswari & Saranya, 2020) DL models can better achieve quicker detections of incident signatures in visual data than traditional image processing methods, more accurately identifying incident signatures in video feeds in real-time. This fast detection capability enables transportation agencies to expedite their dispatch of first responders, address road obstructions to traffic more quickly, and utilise mitigation strategies, such as setting up a diversion, to minimise disturbances to traffic flows. In addition to notifying agencies about incidents to reduce the clearance time of incidents, minimising incident clearance or detection times is a critical aspect used to reduce flow disturbances and secondary accidents that can occur from primary incidents (Lin et al., 2020). (Saleem et al. 2022) With vehicle incidents being detected and alerts going off instantly from video camera feeds via DL, transportation agencies can better monitor vehicular safety and optimise incident management response to transportation networks (Yijing et al., 2023).

Hypothesis

Deep learning models excel at learning complicated spatio-temporal patterns and are useful when applied to real-time traffic congestion prediction. The fact that traffic forecasting, as a classification and regression task, may benefit from deep learning models is due to the mapping of input features to the accurate target output.

Mathematically,

$$O_c = h(x, \theta_c), \qquad O_c \in Z$$

where x represents the input feature vector (vehicle count, vehicle type, movement patterns, temperature, humidity), O_cDenotes the congestion class, θ_c is the set of parameters learned by the hypothesis h, and Z is a set of congestion categories (e.g., low, medium, high).

In this work, a hypothesis function *h* is created to map all traffic-related input features, together with video-based data and other contextual variables, to the correct congestion class or congestion level. The goal of learning the hypothesis is to minimise generalisation error, such that predictions made using unseen traffic data are considered reliable and accurate.

Deep learning models have shown strong abilities to identify complex spatio-temporal distributions of observed values in real-world datasets. In the case of predicting traffic congestion, deep learning can be used to learn from a variety of inputs, including high-dimensional types of input, including measurements of vehicle count, vehicle type, movement patterns, and various environmental factors (e.g., temperature, humidity, etc.). As denoted, forecasting traffic is a classification and regression problem; it is therefore reasonable to assume that a useful learning function h can learn to map a multidimensional input feature vector x to traffic congestion class O c ∈ Z, where Z are discrete traffic congestion classes (e.g., low, medium, high). The goal of learning is to minimise generalisation error so that the system is capable of sound performance on known data and behaves reliably in real-time under previously unheard-of conditions.

It is then expected that an ensemble approach, which utilises multiple learning paradigms and their complementary strengths to make predictions, outperforms a single model. Various learning models may specialise in identifying a form of relationship in the traffic data, whether those are spatial features, temporal interactions, or nonlinear complexities. Aggregating predictions from a variety of models is expected to improve the robustness while reducing overfitting in the predictions for both accuracy and reliability in predicting congestion. This is predicated on an assumption that the combination of complementary learning techniques will offset the vulnerabilities of a single model, with consequent improvement in a better, more generalizable system for real-time prediction and classification of traffic congestion.

1.1 Background

Rapid urbanisation is putting pressure on traditional road networks that cannot handle the increasing number of vehicle users. There are currently 230 million vehicles that are registered, and still growing. It has gotten precarious at this point. There is heterogeneity of vehicle users of motorised vehicles, users of non-motorised vehicles (e.g., bicycles), pedestrian users (walking), and free roaming animals (stray dogs), etc, that mix of actors/agents that is the congestion tends to favour a decrease in overall effective transportation. Many urbanised areas are dealing with inadequate infrastructure. Some of the most common inadequacies are narrow roads, inadequate parking, through traffic management, and the un-separated route of motorised traffic into the public transportation system. In many rapidly urbanising areas, there is not much public transportation available, forcing users to turn to private vehicles. The increasing choice and demand for private vehicles are creating less efficient/blockages, "wasted travel time", and wasted productivity of traffic flows, albeit economic productivity is already low.

In summary, time is wasted for users, lower productivity results in increased stress of travel, economic inefficiencies increase the stress related to all travel, and even air and noise pollution affect the health of the individual user in the area of cardiovascular diseases. With increased stress and economic wastage from delay (lost fuel and time), better understand if the transportation system is already inefficient, and the negative effects on transportation are a form of economic cost and waste. Urbanisation is a challenge because it requires smart traffic management that adheres to big data and models developed on data analytics and machine learning, and deep learning systems (Nallaperuma et al., 2019).

Traffic congestion is not unique to urban regions and is a common problem for urbanising countries around the world. Daily challenges of urban transitioning are stressful/demanding in many parts of the world; much of it, of course, is about adapting to the urban landscape compared to the rural, and is fit for building infrastructure development. Road networks are mature, yet face high levels of congestion. Typical constraints induce congestion, bottlenecks of traffic flow, a lack of alternatives to private vehicle ownership, and problems with urban planning. In congested developing urban cities, developing countries have urban sprawl due to private car usage hustling as there have yet to be any improvements in public transit. The urbanised areas are straining urban mobility systems.

Globally, traffic congestion has increased travel time, economic impacts of supply (logs not cheaper/timely), increased emissions (breathing and carbon), and reduced quality of living standards due to the routines. Policymakers at all levels of government decision-making are increasingly using big data and analytics because Policymakers improve traffic flows and ultimately management. (Procopiou & Chen, 2021) Predictive modelling based on machine learning and deep learning study models improves traffic and is a way to profile congestion patterns, moderating (real-time) or advancing (long-term planning) are two areas of need. For example, Atta et al. (2020) designed an adaptive traffic control system to alter signal timings in real time based on traffic controls in one instance that would improve congestion using an intelligent approach.

This thesis work proposes to outline an approach to a data-smart method that could be beneficial to both developing and developed contexts. This work is tested using Bengaluru as a case study; however, the methodology, including the discursive ensemble and deep learning/data-driven approach, has been applied over a formal study period. The method identifies congestion patterns, detects changes or manipulations in traffic flow elements, and has combinatorial utility for valid or permitted traffic disturbances, more generally for other cities with urban traffic patterns characterised by congestion. The approach is useful for decision-making of microlevel (real-time) traffic management, and macrolevel (strategic urban planning), to long-term (policy level) smart city development, easy to use and not exclusive to one national context, rather it has global relevance, contributing towards cleaner, fairer, and efficient urban transport systems.

1.1.1 Composition of Traffic Participants

In developed nations, chaos results from a uniformity across traffic participants (e.g., vehicles are usually cars, buses, and trucks that use the road in disciplined lanes), and all cities' traffic mix is mostly heterogeneous. The road space is shared by: Private motor vehicles: cars, two-wheelers (motorcycles, scooters), SUVs, Public transport: buses, taxis, auto-rickshaws, and app-based cab services, Commercial vehicles: trucks, delivery vans, tempos, non-motorised vehicles: bicycles, cycle rickshaws, pushcarts, handcarts and Pedestrians, including elderly people, children, and vendors. Also, animals (driven carts, stray animals, especially in rural and semi-urban areas). This heterogeneous mix results in vehicles of very different speeds, sizes, and behaviour, hence resulting in a chaos that is difficult to coordinate, model, and anticipate using traditional methods.

1.1.2 Deployment of Intelligent Traffic Management Systems (ITMS) in Cities

Intelligent Traffic Management Systems (ITMS) have garnered attention in metro cities in India, including Delhi, Bengaluru, Mumbai, and Hyderabad. These systems utilise advanced technologies, including sensors, video cameras, artificial intelligence (AI), and data analytics, to monitor, manage, and optimise traffic flow, public safety, and support wider smart city developments.

Key features of ITMS have included Automatic Number Plate Recognition (ANPR), now used mainly by law enforcement (Jawale et al., 2023), Red Light Violation detection (RLVD) for enforcement of traffic rules, Speed Violation Detection systems (SVDS) for measuring vehicle speed, and round-the-clock surveillance using CCTV cameras. Previously, authors such as Agrawal et al. (2022), Tanwar et al. (2021), and Pustokhina et al. (2020) proposed automated systems that detect and recognise the license plates of commercial trucks in a population; their applications could include weighbridge management. These automotive systems combine image processing and optical character recognition (OCR) methods to remove human bias and improve accuracy (Menon et al., 2018; Khush, 2017).

In addition, Emergency Vehicle Management Systems quicken the movement of ambulances by updating traffic signals. Moreover, emergency predictive models such as machine learning (ML) have been used for congestion analysis to inform routing efficiencies (Soom et al., 2024). City-specific case studies demonstrate different implementations of ITMS. Delhi has implemented AI-based systems to support law enforcement and pollution tracking. Bengaluru employs various Adaptive Traffic Control Systems (ATCS) complemented by various CCTV systems. Mumbai has initiated the Traffic Improvement Project (MITRA) to better monitor safety and behaviour, and Hyderabad's Intelligent Policing System (IPS) now integrates mobile applications for the public to follow road conditions.

Adaptive Traffic Signal Control Systems (ATCS) can respond to real-time vehicle counts and videos and adjust signal times according to the counts, time of day, weather, traffic accidents, and other events or inclement conditions, to increase roadway traffic efficiency and reduce roadway congestion. ATCS has demonstrated major improvements in traffic conditions, including improving roadway outputs, reducing delays, and reducing emissions worsened by stop-and-go traffic conditions. A MFFA (many-factors-for-adaptive) traffic management study in cities such as Delhi, Bengaluru, and Pune says that ATCS could improve the effectiveness and all variables of roadway traffic, should reward road users and turn them into more sustainable road users (Zheng et al., 2019; Zheng, 2022).

There are many variations in vehicle detection and monitoring, including inductive loop detectors, radar, and video detection and analytics. These involve not just the detection of vehicles but monitoring of behaviour, monitoring of traffic, traffic enforcement, incident detection and reporting, and many other safety measures that contribute to improved road safety (Agrawal & Joshi, 2022).

Real-time routing and navigation applications such as Google Maps and Waze provide live routing based on real-time congestion and even accidents. Further, these applications could reduce travel delays and congestion, fuel savings, and reduce congestion and delays could indirectly support public transit and emergency vehicle function. In sum, challenges over the implementation, or adoption, of ITMS remain for the majority of vehicular travel users, particularly in lower accessible tier-2 and tier-3 cities grappling with their own infrastructure and operational issues (Veres & Moussa, 2019). Barriers to efficient ITMS deployments include high capital input for implementation, underdeveloped data connectivity, insufficient standards, data privacy concerns, and low acceptance or awareness of ICT. Additionally, anthropological behaviours driving product demand for new vehicle models reveal that, when appropriately quantified, industry stakeholders continue to disrupt sustainable traffic volumes through an unsustainable transport modality approach (Charef et al., 2022); this makes managing networks harder for advanced traffic ITMS measures.

In that regard, Charef et al. (2022) proposed a smart action system to help systematically better manage to respond to emergency calls, attracting police, fire and ambulance partners towards the emerging ICT offers in improving mobility speed to help arrive at better route choices, while at the same time improving times in a state of emergency for ambulances.

1.1.3 The Rising Concern of Traffic Congestion

For urban cities around the world, traffic congestion is a significant problem. Although urban cities are developing and expanding rapidly, due to higher numbers of vehicles on the road, there are now more breakdowns in traffic flow. As a result of these issues, commuters are spending longer hours sitting in traffic and rising travel costs due to a bonus added to overall travel expenses. In addition to the stress of commuting, traffic congestion tends to result in higher levels of air quality pollutants, which impact the health of urban dwellers. Besides this potential health challenge, traffic congestion will impede the movement and delivery of goods and services, which impacts economic efficiency.

For more metropolitan cities that subscribe to urban road development, with an insufficient number of road segments and cannot provide enough parking for users, there are almost no lanes for public transportation or even lanes for non-motorised travel. With so many infrastructure challenges, there are greater "costs associated with congestion", and getting around the city effectively is diminished.

Traffic congestion creates gains and losses beyond optimal travel times. The extended exposure to air and noise pollution, since drivers sit consumed in traffic, has been linked to respiratory and cardiovascular diseases (Papathanasopoulou et al., 2022). Sitting idling in traffic generates more emissions of greenhouse gases, creating a possible problem for environmental pollution. Traffic congestion also creates "compounding risk issues" as the high frequency of stop-and-go limits the opportunity for inducing safer drivers, while there is a greater risk for accidents. Pedestrian and cyclist behaviour increases the risk at busy intersections, as both are vulnerable road users.

Following the challenges of traffic congestion, there is an impetus for good planning and management of traffic systems for urban mobility. Planners and/or public policy makers must look to innovative paths and pursue opportunities, besides deterministic interpretations of urban mobility; the end goal should be a sustainable and livable city.

1.1.4 Growth of Traffic and Its Effects on Cities

Worldwide, city traffic has increased in the past two decades in large part due to rapid urbanisation, increasing incomes, and increasing urban populations. This increase in traffic has unsettled traditional structures of urban transportation based on historical assumptions regarding how cities expand and how people travel. The conversion of the urban population towards increasing reliance on the use of personal vehicles, specifically two-wheelers and cars, has also contributed to traffic build-up. Public transport use has declined, and many cities have deficient levels of public transport, even though private vehicle ownership is mandatory for many households. The issue of having more than 230 million registered vehicles within the country and increases in vehicle densities, particularly in urban areas, leads to major mismatches in approved infrastructure, mostly due to incompatible infrastructure, such as narrow streets leading to illegal street parking, and no dedicated lanes for adequate bus services or non-motorised modes of travel. All of this leads to greater travel times, frequent bottlenecks, and delays, leading to not only greater road rage and traffic fines but also lower average travel speeds, mainly within central business district areas.

The outcomes of congestion are not just delays and inconvenience; the analysis also has economic, environmental, and public health consequences. Productivity losses are incredible; it's billions of rupees lost every year in vehicles idling, fuel, and delivery time, specifically because of being stuck in traffic. The increased number of vehicles is contributing to severe levels of air and noise pollution, leading to health-related problems, e.g., respiratory problems, cardiovascular diseases, particularly for the most vulnerable in society. Furthermore, cities are facing a safety crisis with a high level of incidence of road traffic accidents and their impacts on pedestrians, cyclists, and two-wheeled vehicle users. Cities typically look towards urban planning and policy solutions, which are often reactive and/or short-term. Urban planning often looks to simply expand road networks and build flyovers; these solutions do not consider unplanned sprawl, insufficient last-mile connectivity, and a lack of integrated land use and transportation planning. An ensemble deep learning technique for predicting traffic congestion is proposed, and using historical data and real-time data, as well as contextual conditions such as overall weather and traffic patterns, supports a new data-driven movement towards a higher-quality urban mobility system that is economic, efficient, and sustainable.

1.2 Motivation for the Study

Traffic congestion has become an important problem in areas where the urban population can grow rapidly. Traffic congestion is an issue that affects millions of commuters every day. Urbanisation and the growing habit of private ownership of motor vehicles in all communities, from small to large, have produced a saturated road network, particularly in large metropolitan areas such as Delhi, Mumbai, Bengaluru, and Chennai. Despite attempts by government agencies to mitigate congestion through a variety of initiatives, traditional traffic management strategies and rule-based systems have not been able to substantially reduce congestion. Based on personal observations and research based on traffic datasets, the daily observation of congestion every day with long queues of vehicles at traffic intersections, unreliable travel times, and visible commuter irritation has not only been personally challenging but has also sparked intellectual motivation to investigate the issue further. This is a particularly large problem in developing countries, where the demand for urban mobility is growing at a rate that will exceed the supply and transport infrastructure for a rapidly urbanising population.

The urgent need for intelligent, data-driven approaches that fully learns from complex traffic behaviours and the capability to provide timely predictions is here. Technologies involving Artificial Intelligence (AI), Machine Learning (ML), and Deep Learning (DL) similarly provide a new frontier for feasible predictive traffic management systems (Taherifard et al., 2019). Advanced models are more effective than traditional statistical methods at identifying patterns in large datasets with complex, non-linear relationships. By using millions of historical data points and incorporating real-time traffic information, these models provide more accurate and valuable insights for traffic analysis. Specifically, ensemble learning methods, which create multiple base learners to improve the predictive performance of a single model, are already showing promise. Some of the methods proposed (as noted earlier) are stacking ensemble methods, which utilise a meta-learner to synthesise the outputs of the selected base model (Lu, M et al., 2023). Stacking ensemble methods remains the best at capturing certain patterns or characteristics in the data for superior input into the meta-learner stage. This study is fueled by the promises stacking strategy could offer within the field of traffic, particularly to provide a more accurate, scalable, and robust system of predicting traffic congestion (Bokaba et al.,2022).

In addition to that, numerous studies have been conducted internationally to assess traffic forecasting with various machine learning methods; however, not much attention has been paid to the various complex and, at times, polemic traffic conditions that exist in many countries. Mixed vehicle types, unstructured driving, jaywalking, lack of lane discipline, and poorly synchronised public transport systems contribute to traffic being volatile and very turbulent. In this regard, regional studies with local datasets are required to provide tailored and appropriate means of development to cater to traffic management solutions.

Thus, this study is motivated by the objective to contribute not only to the body of academic knowledge but also to explore a perceptible, real-world solution that will serve traffic authorities, urban planners, and smart city efforts resulting in a simulated amalgamation of traffic that quickens traffic flow, reduces congestion, saves time for commuters, and lessens the negative environmental impact - making the cities more live able and efficient.

1.3 Problem Statement

Traffic flow forecasting is fundamentally a time series prediction problem. This follows from the assumption that the congestion levels observed in preceding states influence the subsequent congestion levels. Thus, one must maintain the temporal continuity of the data to apply the prediction model appropriately. This research utilises traffic flow data derived from video data (Yang, X. et al., 2022). The temporal features are found from sequences of video frames, and the spatial features are derived from object detection (vehicle count, location, etc.). Because the data over time will change, the prediction target at the time step Tn Becomes highly relevant for prediction T_{n+1} . Single-step predictions are used when the model predicts a single target value for a particular time for future movements, while multi-step prediction refers to when the model forecasts multiple future values for the respective consecutive time intervals (Cini and Aydin, 2024).

In Equations 1 and 2, Let F_t The traffic flow feature is extracted at time t. The spatial-temporal feature matrix could be constructed by merging multiple video segments seen over time for their corresponding values as follows:

$$F_t = \begin{bmatrix} f_1^1 & f_2^1 & f_3^1 & \cdots & f_t^1 \\ f_1^2 & f_2^2 & f_3^2 & \cdots & f_t^2 \\ \vdots & \vdots & \vdots & \ddots & \vdots \\ f_1^n & f_2^n & f_3^n & \cdots & f_t^n \end{bmatrix} \qquad (1)$$

In this case, n is the number of video segments (clips), with each row representing chronological flow features for one video segment and columns representing different time steps. Then frame the forecasting problem with a look-back window. α To forecast traffic conditions in the future over a prediction horizon sized h. The model learns a mapping function θ, which maps the observations to their future outcome in the following way.

$$\begin{bmatrix} f_{t-\alpha} \\ f_{t-(\alpha-1)} \\ f_{t-(\alpha-2)} \\ \vdots \\ f_{t-1} \end{bmatrix} \xrightarrow[\theta]{\left(\begin{smallmatrix}\text{mapping} \\ \text{function}\end{smallmatrix}\right)} \begin{bmatrix} f_t \\ f_{t+1} \\ f_{t+2} \\ \vdots \\ f_{t+(h-1)} \end{bmatrix} \qquad (2)$$

Where: f_t traffic flow feature at a time, α number of look-back steps (historical time steps used for prediction), h Prediction horizon (number of future steps to be predicted), θ learned mapping function (e.g., ensemble deep learning model).

This mathematical formulation provides the basis for developing a predictive model that describes spatial and temporal dependencies using video-based traffic data. The features extracted using block-based feature extraction methods will be used as inputs to ensemble models combining deep learning and traditional learners to improve prediction accuracy and robustness across different traffic conditions.

1.4 Research Objectives

These objectives are proposed here to address the complicated nature of traffic congestion by applying modern machine learning approaches and various sets of data. The research will not only develop models but also qualitatively evaluate them to provide useful insights and workable solutions for better traffic management in the urban environment.

The key objectives of the research are

- To develop a predictive model that can accurately forecast traffic congestion patterns based on historical traffic data and current traffic data, weather conditions, and other relevant factors.
- Evaluate the performance of the ensemble learning approach against other existing methods for traffic congestion prediction
- Identifying the object related to the traffic system and identifying the patterns for forecasting traffic congestion.

1.5 Research Design

In order to successfully reach the research aims, it was critical to develop a clear and systematic research design. The research design provided a sequential and systematic walk-through of the study, from data collection to model building and prediction. The sections that follow will present the research design and the approach followed throughout the study. This research topic was chosen in consideration of a genuine and current problem. Traffic congestion is a common problem in the world today. (Williams et al., 2022) Urban travel has become challenging because of an increase in the number of vehicles, reduction in infrastructure expansion, and large number of people living in urban areas that make many individuals operate long distances with long delays, a lack of relevance to when many people prefer to go (such as work shifts or flexible hours), and more recently, extensive stress associated with travel times.

The common nature of traffic congestion in modern urban life compelled the study to examine the creation of a predictive traffic congestion model from video data and machine learning through the analysis of various ways people monitor or become aware of congestion (Tsalikidis et al., 2024). The first stage of the study involved a lot of general reading about traffic, including the concepts of traffic flow, traffic rules, causes of congestion, and patterns in urban mobility. Looked at everything traffic-related in one capacity or another and paid particular attention to the current technologies being used for traffic monitoring and congestion analysis. As this stage of the study moved along, many research papers were considered to consider the various methods, tools, and datasets that had all been previously used.

Figure 1: Research Design for Traffic Congestion Prediction

Figure 1 depicts the general research approach employed for traffic congestion prediction. It starts with collecting the video data from camera footage and extracting the frames with OpenCV. Once the frames are extracted, object detection is performed, and features are extracted (multiple features, including weather data). The features were then passed into the base models (MLP, SVC, CNN-LSTM), and predictions were made using the stacked ensemble with a meta learner to classify the traffic congestion level.

Once the literature review was conducted, the next step was to decide upon the data collection method. After consideration of multiple styles of data collection, it was determined that real-time video footage would provide the highest level of accuracy and wealth of data. Given the interest in video-based data collection, the Habbal flyover was selected for collection due to its known high traffic density. Furthermore, video data was to be filmed whilst the area was at capacity, thereby maximising the variety in operating conditions, including congestion level on the day of video collection (Zheng, J., 2018). Not surprisingly, managing large video files was challenging. As a result of the high resolution of the videos, processing them required substantial computing power and frequently crashed or were delayed in downloading files before completing. To simplify matters, VLC media player was used to break the full video into shorter, appropriate clips for further data processing.

In either case, the YOLOv8 (You Only Look Once version 8) object detection model was used because of its efficiency (speed) and accuracy with multiple types of object detection (Liu et al., 2024; Guo & Zhang, 2022). As a result, it was complemented with (CNN) techniques using the images of the frames to extract features from them (Zhang, H. et al.,2022). Finally, the data from above was still to be used to produce a firm congestion prediction model. During this entire process, the existing research articles and experiments were numerous and led to continuous learning, modification, and refining of the methodology of the entire project. The final research model stemmed from a combination of applying deep learning and ensemble mixed models to maximise both accuracy and feasibility in the real world (Rangari, A. P. et al., 2022).

The research approach to this study is based on developing and examining an ensemble deep-learning model to predict traffic congestion outcomes. This ensemble, called Ensemble Deep Learning Model (EDLM), will utilise video data collected from traffic scenes and incorporate several sophisticated feature extraction methods, such as object detection and weather data (Tsalikidis, N. et al. 2024). The base learners in the model will be CNN-LSTM for capturing spatiotemporal patterns (Song et al., 2022), MLP for pattern learning, and SVC for constraining the decision boundary. Logistic Regression will be the meta learner for the base models' outputs to establish the final congestion classification. The approach is for the methods to be supervised learning, data processing, developing features, cross-validation, etc. The sequencing is concluded by the analysis of large datasets of traffic congestion prediction through data.

1.6 Description of the Implemented Model

Urbanisation in countries and the growing number of vehicles were exacerbating congestion problems in metropolitan cities and causing severe complications to users, transport authorities, and urban planners. The lack of effective traffic forecasting systems leads to longer and more unreliable travel times, excessive fuel consumption, and further degradation of the environment. However, current traffic prediction techniques, especially those based on traditional machine learning algorithms, cannot appropriately track the changing nature and spatial and temporal dependencies of real-world traffic data.

This research is designed to counteract these shortcomings by proposing an ensemble deep learning model capable of intuitive and real-time traffic congestion forecasting. The main aim was to create an observable, robust, scalable framework that is data-driven, while being able to assemble heterogeneous features generated through video surveillance, object detection, and contextual weather information. The model used in this thesis combined the complementary benefits of different deep learning and machine learning-based models, including a Convolutional Neural Network with Long Short-Term Memory (CNN-LSTM) deep learning model, a Multilayer Perceptron (MLP), and a Support Vector Classifier (SVC) as the base learners. With this choice of model, it is possible to have these 3 separate models trained on different aspects of the traffic dataset, thus still considering spatial-temporal dynamics and nonlinear trends while understanding the outputs as a unique prediction (generated from a learned process).

The final ensemble predictions were aggregated using Logistic Regression as the meta-learner, resulting in a single ensemble prediction output. The entire architecture was implemented with a structured training pipeline, processing the video frames for object detection, extracting features, and fusing with external weather parameters. As an ensemble deep learning strategy, a stacking strategy was used, allowing for improved overall generalisation and superior predictive accuracy over any individual models.

The process continues with collecting traffic video data from several selected intersections, then extracting the video into individual frames for object detection of vehicles and other traffic entities. The main features, such as the count of objects, object type, movement patterns, and environmental data (temperature, humidity, and narrative of the weather), are extracted. For each object count, type, and movement, the features and structure are pooled in a dataset format that is usable for training. Preprocessing is performed to ensure the reduction of noise, temporal alignment, normalisation of input features, and label features as required. Then, the ensemble deep learning model is trained and validated using the video labelled traffic datasets, as well as performance is compared to many traditional models, including Linear Regression, Decision Tree, Random Forest, K-Nearest Neighbours, and Support Vector Regressor. The experimental results showed that the ensemble deep learning framework was significantly more accurate and resilient than the level of traffic congestion predictions among the models used.

The ensemble deep learning framework utilised video-based visual features and weather context, allowing the model to properly recognise dynamic behaviours within the traffic system, as contrasted with previous models. MAE, MSE, RMSE, and R^2 score - comparative evaluation metrics provided reasonable evidence but not certitude that levels of traffic congestion predictions could leverage increased prediction power using short-term and midterm forecasts. This study concluded that ensemble deep learning models provide an efficient and flexible modelling approach to traffic congestion predictions in smart cities.

Ensemble deep learning models are more efficient and flexible because the authors can accommodate many varied types of data sources and learn complex time-varying patterns concurrently, making them perfect candidates for deployment in real time. Future work includes deploying this model with an advanced intelligent transportation system (ITS), streaming live data, monitoring for congestion across the city, and possibly proactively controlling traffic congestion in real-time, city-wide. Since this model uses vast amounts of data, adding analytical capabilities concerning network topology of the roadways via data feeds from GPS, mobile sensors, and social-media analytics will better inform the operational reality and the potential impacts or influence on traffic congestion.

1.7 Scope of the Study

This research focuses on traffic congestion prediction through an ensemble deep learning model that uses several data modalities, including historical traffic patterns, contemporaneous weather data, and video-based traffic descriptors (Zhang, T. et al., 2023). The goal is to ultimately provide a reliable solution that can be deployed and adapted across diverse traffic conditions, including highly urban environments with heavy traffic patterns and rural spaces with less organised traffic patterns.

This study primarily employs multi-modal traffic data using an ensemble model that combines Convolutional Neural Network with Long Short-Term Memory (CNN-LSTM), Multi-Layer Perceptron (MLP), and Support Vector Classifier (SVC) models. The ensemble method takes advantage of the individual models' strengths to train an ensemble model that captures the temporal, spatial, and non-linear attributes of traffic flow to provide predictive capability. The ensemble model increases predictive ability and predictive robustness (Awan, A. A., et al., 2024).

In addition, the research highlights the valuable applicability of video footage in traffic studies by extracting and using frames that contain traffic information, detecting moving objects, and applying advanced feature engineering to encapsulate a real-time aspect of traffic pattern learning. Furthermore, the consideration for congestion using real-time weather variables adds another layer to the model's utility, helping authorities predict congestion management from various weather contexts (Zhang, D., et al., 2018). Ultimately, this research has moved towards realising scalable intelligent traffic management systems that improve efficiency in daily commuter travel and enhance long-term planning and environmental outcomes in both metro and non-metro regions of the country.

1.8 Organisation of the Thesis

In this thesis, six main chapters systematically address the different components of the research study related to the problem of traffic congestion prediction using ensemble deep learning. Chapter 1: Introduction. This chapter presents the background of the study, with specific reference to the developing countries' traffic context regarding traffic participants and urban transportation technologies. This chapter also describes the impetus for the study, the problem statement, research objectives, delimitation, and the thesis organisation. Literature Review.

Chapter 2 covers previous research associated with traffic congestion, causes and effects, measurement approaches, and forecasting time series. The literature review also contains information related to the application of machine learning, deep learning, ensemble learning methods (specifically CNN-LSTM, MLP, and SVC), and object detection with a traffic system (e.g., vehicles, congestion). This chapter also ends with the gaps in the literature identified for research.

Chapter 3: Research Methodology. This chapter describes the overall research design, data collection methodology, preprocessing, and feature extraction techniques. The chapter also describes the formulation of the prediction problem, the present study ensemble deep learning model, base and meta-learners, and experimental setup. The chapter further describes the evaluation metrics, implementation tools and technologies, and hardware specifications. Chapter 4: Implementation and Results. The chapter outlines the datasets, whether training or validating the model, and the analysis of individual base learners' performance, and the ensemble model's performance. Furthermore, a comparison with traditional models is made. In addition to this, a comparison is carried out between the developed ensemble model and another existing ensemble method to assess the improvements in prediction performance and robustness. After interpreting the results, including actual vs predicted compared to statistical evidence using ANOVA.

Chapter 5: Discussion. This chapter discusses the main findings along with the contributions of the study to the field, as well as the difficulties faced in conducting this research, and provides a personal reflection on the ramifications of the results.

Chapter 6: Conclusion and Future Work. This chapter indicates the developed methodology, originality, and contributions of the study overall, evaluates how these models performed generally, and lays out the limitations of the study. Lastly, the chapter discusses proposals for future research and the potential for improvement. At the end of the thesis, references and appendices are given, and the appendices are supporting materials such as codes, sample data, and additional figures or tables.

1.9 Summary

The introductory chapter of this dissertation commences within the context of the traffic systems in developing countries, with an emphasis on the unusual challenges posed by diverse traffic, limited infrastructure, and rising vehicle density. It examines who the traffic participants are, while also examining traffic participants' increasing usage of intelligent transportation technologies, especially in urban contexts. It also identifies the growing issue of traffic congestion and describes how the issue of traffic congestion and its negative impacts on economic productivity, environmental sustainability, and human safety. The introduction also identifies how traditional traffic management systems have struggled with adjusting to strategies or frameworks that are dynamic, unstructured, and data-rich due to the nature of traffic in developing countries. The catalyst for this research lies in the pressing need for predictive models that can properly navigate the complexity of traffic conditions in developing countries.

The problem formulation section describes the drawbacks of traditional methods, such as low accuracy, inability to process real-time heterogeneous data, and inability to adjust to unstructured traffic conditions. This chapter outlines the objective of the research, which includes: developing a video-based ensemble deep framing, combining environmental and object-based traffic features, and comparing the developed framing against baseline models. The scope of the research is framed within the urban environment of developing countries, and the chapter concludes with a summary of the thesis structure, thereby anchoring the research presented in the following chapters.

Chapter 2: Literature Review

Traffic congestion is an ongoing issue in metropolitan areas around the globe, particularly in developing countries where urban growth has outpaced the development of transportation infrastructures. To understand this problem, it is important to assess the current traffic prediction processes and systems in place to manage congestion. This can occur through a critical review of prior research studies. A review of previous research studies can help with understanding prior work around algorithms, models, and data types, and the limitations of each of these. Additionally, it can help establish background knowledge of the importance of artificial intelligence in shifting prior research from legacy traffic analysis systems to systems that can use inputs in real time and offer adaptability, functional flexibility, and predictive capabilities.

This chapter reviewed the existing literature around the topic of the present study. First, it established background information on traffic congestion and the many factors that contribute to it. Then, it reviewed important machine learning and deep learning approaches used in traffic prediction work to address congestion, followed by an overview of ensemble learning. The chapter described the recent advancements in object detection for traffic systems, including reviews of the literature involving traffic forecasting using mammalian multimodal data. Lastly, the chapter described research gaps created by other studies that this study will attempt to address.

2.1 Overview of Traffic Congestion

City traffic congestion is a physical matter of great concern everywhere; it is caused by human factors such as population growth, increased individual vehicle ownership, and lagging infrastructure. The effects of congestion are lengthy trips, fuel consumption, emissions affecting air quality, and stressed commuters. The World Health Organisation (2016) demonstrates that cars in congested conditions contribute to deteriorating urban air quality, harming the environment and human health. Urban transportation systems experience high congestion during peak hours from not synchronization between the demand for urban traffic and the available pathways for traffic. Traffic is a dynamic process, complex in nature, that experiences congestion from elevated levels of demand, often exceeding the capacity of traffic roadways, as well as human behaviour, and when combined with accidents, weather, or signal timing, each factor creates further complications. Alam (2025) identified the complexity of listing all potential spatiotemporal factors of AI and ML-based prediction models, and further, the limitations of AI and ML-based modelling for prediction approaches that fail to capture the nonlinear, time-variant nature of an urban traffic system. The findings in said research illustrate the need for new traffic prediction systems that are advanced enough to identify the traffic condition before it happens and can put appropriate responses in place before the usual aftermath occurs.

Given these issues, traffic prediction models are quickly emerging as a common feature in intelligent transportation systems (ITS), which can often be described in their simplest form as forecasting possible congestion levels, noting alternative timings for signals, and directing trip advice to users (Veres, M. et al., 2019). More simply, machine learning (ML) and deep learning (DL) methods can provide value due to their primary advantages of being able to deal with large amounts of data, many different kinds, and no collated information types and sources, recognising patterns, and learning from new data and relevant previous observations. Ultimately, (Savithramma et al. 2022) argue that three of the most used ML algorithms, decision trees, support vector machines, and ensembles, outperform routine statistical techniques concerning prediction.

One key point made in the recent articles, especially the latest review, is that predictive traffic analytics are important because traffic management over the years has pursued traditional traffic movement measures that missed a way to alleviate congestion in today's contemporary free-flowing metropolitan traffic situations. And that fiduciary dependence on any step forward with any machine learning algorithms to underpin forecasting any future flow of traffic in cities and urban centres is more scientifically based and an ideal traffic management practice going forward.

In addition, improvements in technologies related to information and data gathering, such as GPS tracking, traffic observation cameras, and sensors utilising IoT, have produced better traffic management data (Uddin, M. I. et al., 2021). Therefore, there is now an opportunity for both video-based and hybrid systems to measure vehicle density and movement characteristics, and in some instances even the weather, to achieve improved informative congestion predictions. For example, a method to examine congestion in real time, utilising both YOLOv8 for object detection and LSTM networks for sequence prediction, which is an ideal example of how to do this and make a visual method incorporated with other things into a larger and comprehensive traffic prediction pipeline.

Traffic congestion is a growing concern in many developing cities due to urbanisation, increased motorised vehicles, and slow pedestrian infrastructure development (Papathanasopoulou, V. et al., 2022). Compared to cities in the rest of the world, major urban areas, namely Delhi, Mumbai, Bengaluru, and Hyderabad, rank among the cities around the world with the most traffic congestion. Los Angeles, Mexico City, São Paulo, and Jakarta are facing similar challenges of severe and overwhelming congestion, demonstrating that traffic congestion is a global problem for both developing and developed areas. All cities are essentially at the top of every traffic index for congestion across the globe. Numerous factors result in congestion—roads are narrow, there are encroachments, mixed traffic with two and four-wheel motor vehicles, auto-rickshaws, as well as unknown pedestrian road-crossing/movement. (TomTom, 2023) The TomTom Traffic Index (2023) shows that congestion proliferates, with commuters wasting millions of hours week after week on congested roads, resulting in lost economic hours for others and lost ecologies for the environment.

System traffic (especially in urban areas) is subject to specific operational challenges because of the informal nature of traffic behaviour through the limited understanding and adoption of state-of-the-art adaptive traffic control systems (Uddin, M. I. et al., 2021). While many western countries have many established traffic patterns with lane discipline and the use of traffic sensors and detectors integrated on moderate to high-density roads, most roadways in developing countries have no regard for lane structure, often experience illegal parking, and work in a poorly enforced environment. Hence, there is an emergent need for advanced traffic surveillance and predictive models that can handle noisy, unstructured, and multimodal data inputs. For example, the Central Road Research Institute (CRRI) and Indian Institutes of Technology (IITs) have suggested that accurate congestion prediction and forecasting are essential for urban traffic management, but equally useful for emergency vehicle routing and public transport scheduling.

Recent innovations in intelligent transportation systems (ITS) have resulted in a wealth of opportunities for Indian smart cities to begin using AI and related approaches for traffic forecasting. With the expansion of surveillance infrastructure through initiatives such as the Smart Cities Mission, new sources of real-time traffic video data are being made available for analysis. Data can be used to inform very contextual prediction models that detect traffic flows and movements when data is combined with environmental data (weather, visibility, and/or air quality). And combining video analytics-based methods with machine learning can provide better accuracy in often congested city traffic settings.

Furthermore, accurate congestion predictions will enable authorities to implement adaptive rerouting of vehicles in real time, using real-time notifications to commuters and dynamic systems to adapt the signals (Mystakidis et al., 2024). Active traffic management is important in everyday road management but even more vital during periods of high demand, such as public events, rallies of political groups populated by tens of thousands of individuals, congregations of potential worshippers by faith organisations, and holiday travel (Wang, C. et al., 2025). Given the variability of demand context, there is even an opportunity to integrate hybrid models based on ensemble learning, connecting many approaches of base learners to develop a better prediction reliability and engage to learn in adaptive real-time traffic conditions. To this end, this research describes a new framework of stacking ensemble learning in the prediction of traffic congestion in real-time urban environments, as are typically described, while also engaging both numerical and video-based learner features (Rasaizadi, M. et al., 2022).

Furthermore, despite work being noted in this space, adaptive systems are still missing from many urban areas for traffic congestion management (Ding et al., 2021). In tandem with the evidence of this study, there is the ongoing need for the development of models that integrate structured descriptive numerical data (eg, vehicle counts, timestamps) with video analytics and even fused with environment data to allow active learning (Dai et al., 2019). While the foundations are meaningful, the other motivation of these integrations was not only for improved accuracy but also for resilience to the automatic complexity of urban habitats and for improved capacity to scale with the growth of cities. Therefore, integrated or multilevel prediction systems are required for innovation in smart cities and for sustainable urban mobility (Duan et al., 2019; Duan et al., 2021).

2.1.1 Causes of Traffic Congestion

Traffic congestion in urban and semi-urban contexts is a function of infrastructure, vehicles, behaviour, and, to some extent, external factors. Infrastructure limitations are a significant cause of congestion, especially where road systems have not expanded with the increase in vehicle numbers, as is the case in many developing environments where the roads fail to keep pace with rising demand, resulting in congestion as well as inefficiencies (Tsalikidis et al., 2024; Ding et al., 2025). Road systems suffer from inadequate capacity and geometric design; lane-dedicated public transport is often lacking; and traffic signals often fail to be synchronised. One of the most central reasons for congestion is the rapidly increasing number of vehicles per individual, with the growth in private vehicle use being particularly significant. These numbers exceed the carrying capacity of the road, which leads to greater congestion during peak periods due to the space constraints, which are more conducive to congestion in slow-moving vehicles (Bogaerts et al., 2020). These trends are indeed similar to trends in traffic management systems that often ignore the dynamic nature of peak-hour demands (Zhang et al., 2025).

Al-Heety et al. (2022) developed a traffic congestion control system with a situational awareness component and communication infrastructure for the traffic agents that would improve system and agent performance while emergency events are occurring. The system implements an agent utilising reinforcement learning and a non-dominated sorting genetic algorithm to alleviate areas of congestion and improve overall traffic flow before the emergency event. An even larger contributor towards inhibiting traffic flow is behavioural. This includes improper lane usage areas of high show of not only lane changing but lane changing immediately next to another vehicle's lane (Qu et al., 2019; Wang, S.B., et al., 2024). Congestion is compounded with illegally parked vehicles, roadside parking, and unplanned pedestrian crossings blocking the effective use of the road width, and temporal instabilities (Do et al., 2019).

External and environmental factors impact congestion as well; these include bad weather, road work (maintenance), accidents, and vehicles breaking down in the traffic corridor. In combination, these impacts all promote congestion both directly, through sudden and unforeseen reductions in carrying capacity, and indirectly through the reaction and feedback mechanisms associated with them as individuals make decisions in their travel alternatives after congestion occurs. Given the many causes and uncertainties, modern traffic management systems must find adaptive strategies using predictive modelling (Shanmugam, A. et al., 2024). Ensemble learning techniques have been advocated to improve the accuracy and robustness of congestion prediction models operating under a varying environment (Chen et al., 2020).

Thus, the complexity, compounded by the dynamic nature of congestion, is a consideration for the planning and management of traffic systems and their environments. Traffic congestion will remain for the foreseeable future as the inevitable outcome of combining infrastructure, behaviours, maintainability-based environments, and forthcoming data-driven solutions into actions that can mitigate longer-standing operations.

2.1.2 Effects of Traffic Congestion

Traffic congestion has produced a slew of negative impacts on sustainable urban systems. Public health and the environment, as well as economic outcomes, all suffer from traffic congestion. A large body of urban planning and transportation research documents these effects. Economically, traffic congestion has created high costs in the form of less travel time, less productivity, and higher transportation costs. Delays in transporting goods and services impede supply chains, reducing overall economic efficiency. The increased stop-and-go traffic has added to fuel consumption rates, thereby increasing economic costs for both the private and commercial vehicle operators.

There has also been an increase in pollutant emissions, for example, particulates (PM), nitrogen oxides (NOx), and carbon monoxide (CO), from frequent accelerations/decelerations and extended idling times, which have negatively affected air quality in congested urban corridors. The quantity of air pollution emitted creates a riskier situation for air quality deterioration. There are evident public health ramifications. Traffic congestion is associated with heart disease, stress-related illnesses, and respiratory illnesses associated with high vehicle emissions. Traffic congestion has likewise affected the quality of life and mental well-being associated with noise pollution caused by congested streets. Similarly, on a social basis, traffic congestion inhibits accessibility to critical services, increases travel times, and decreases the reliability of public transit. These factors impede work-life balance and create less livable cities. Furthermore, frequent lane changes and aggressive driving increase the likelihood of a collision in highly dense environments. Traffic safety has also declined. Complexity and unpredictability in urban environments have created complications for emergency responders and delay times for traffic management.

2.1.3 Methods for Measuring Congestion

An abundance of methods has been developed and implemented to measure traffic congestion in various ways, providing information on its intensity, duration, and spatial distribution. These methods have provided great benefits to planning, performance evaluation, and transportation management plan development.

Time-Based Measures of Travel. Travel time has traditionally been regarded as the most apparent congestion measure. Measuring distances based on travel times has been widely used using measures like the Travel Time Index (TTI) and Buffer Time Index (BTI) (Huang et al., 2018). The Travel Time Index is the ratio of travel time during the AM or PM peak hours relative to the travel time based on free-flow conditions. The Buffer Time Index is a measure of the additional time needed to arrive when there is variation in travel speeds and to be on time (Abdelbaki et al., 2022). Measures Based on Speed. Average speed and speed variance have also been used as indicators of congestion; it was suggested that more traffic had the effect of lowering the average speed in comparison to the posted speed limit (Sahu et al., 2024). Speed data from common road sensors and GPS-enabled devices has enabled real-time congestion monitoring and congestion mapping. V/C ratio, or volume-to-capacity ratio. The V/C ratio has a long history of being used as an industry standard to assess how "saturated" a road segment is. Traffic engineering interprets a value near or greater than 1.0 as suggesting that traffic demand has exceeded road capacity, and therefore, high levels of congestion exist.

Service Level, or LOS, qualitatively measures traffic operating conditions (and is typically categorised from A- free-flowing conditions to F- highly congested conditions). Considerations of speed, travel time, traffic jams, and comfort have all been included in LOS. Measures Based on Delays. Congestion measures have also been based on delays, considering the difference between ideal travel times versus actual travel times (World Health Organisation, 2016). Typical measures of the effects of congestion on commuters and logistics systems have included average delay per vehicle and total person-hours of delay. Length of Queue and Stop Time. Average stop time and length of queuing have also been operational indicators of congestion that have been helpful for short-term signal optimisation states and are often collected from camera feeds, loop detectors, or by observation. The choice of congestion measure has been largely dependent upon the availability of data, intended purpose, and scope of the analysis. In recent years, the advent of real-time data sources, data analytics, and machine learning has combined to create a more accurate and useful congestion measurement framework.

2.1.4 Techniques for Identifying and Forecasting Congestion

Now that congestion detection and prediction are fundamental to controlling use of modern traffic networks, congestion detection and prediction could offer rapid responses to congestion, foresight into growing traffic volumes, and confirmation of the condition of roadways. This largely includes many methods with varying models and technologies, merging leading-edge data-driven technology with conventional traffic engineering, such as Sensor-Based Detection, GPS and Probe Vehicle Data, Data Fusion, Machine Learning Models, Deep Learning Methods, Simulation-Based Methods, and Hybrid Systems.

Seated sensors, such as roadside cameras, inductive loops, or infrared detectors, have and will often be used for monitoring lane occupancy, vehicle speeds, and volumes of traffic. To gain continuous data to measure observed congestion, these systems are more likely to be located on highly trafficked roads and intersections. For instance, through these means, qualitative data is collected just as well; however, the downside lies in the maintenance schedules and whether or not the user can have the infrastructure (Uddin et al., 2021). More reliable than fixed-location sensors are probe data, GPS-enabled devices in the vehicles, or a smartphone, to measure traffic flows in larger areas. More dependable, because probe data provides both speed and location, which would allow for dynamic congestion detection too, that does not solely depend on sectioned roadway infrastructure. It has been used for things like real-time traffic maps, routing applications, and the most sophisticated traffic control system (Lana et al., 2018).

Analysing disparate data sources for congestion would be sure to increase accuracy, as it would include all data originating from environmental surroundings, historical data, GPS for traffic metrics, and TMCs/ Other Traffic sensors from multiple sources. It allows traffic systems to react more forcefully in a shorter period to sudden changes in traffic behaviour through mixed methods of data fusion, along with simply supplying a more complete view of conditions on the roadway (Do et al, 2019). Machine learning algorithms for congestion prediction can use static traffic data captured through features based on vehicle counts, speed profile, and environmental data to train algorithms, including but not limited to ensemble classifiers, decision trees, and support vector machines. For short-term forecasting of traffic congestion events and in the automated dictates of traffic control (Wang, Z. et al., 2020; N L. N. et al., 2018).

The study can deal with congestion prediction problems through advanced deep learning. Examples include Recurrent Neural Networks (RNN) and Long Short-Term Memory (LSTM) Networks, which would provide more accurate congestion predictions than basic machine learning models, and are especially effective for long-term prediction as well as recognising sequential behaviour of traffic data (Li et al, 2021). Traffic conditions are emulated in both micro and macro simulated environments with traffic simulation tools such as SUMO, VISSIM, Trans Modeller, etc. Furthermore, it provides an opportunity for planners to assess the design of a road network, updates and changes of policies and regulations for traffic, and timing of traffic signalling, etc., before the implementation of a plan. Simulation of traffic conditions allows planners to assess several variations of demand, which will assist in the decision-making process.

Hybrid systems use two or more approaches for congestion detection and prediction. For example, it may have AI-based prediction, simulation models, and real-time data. Hybrid systems offer additional insight into traffic behaviour for traffic control centres to evaluate adaptive signal control and reduce reaction time (Khalil et al., 2024). Hybrid systems are becoming more popular in smart city initiatives. Detecting and predicting based on historical data on traffic flow will be an improved approach to managing traffic within cities. Traffic authorities can ensure improved levels of traffic flow throughout an urban transportation network when the study takes real-time data and prediction capabilities into account (Ganesan et al., 2024). In a U.S. patent, Wang, T., et al. (2023) proposed a method for real-time large-scale traffic flow prediction, specifically fuzzy logic combined with deep LSTM. Li and Park (2023) described an automatic high-beam control system designed for use in autonomous machines. The system improves visibility and reduces glare, helping to provide safer navigation in different lighting conditions.

2.2 Machine Learning and Deep Learning Techniques

Deep learning and machine learning go hand in hand as fundamental components of intelligent traffic management systems. Concerning urban transport networks, it is likely that these will be used to predict blocked traffic, model uncertain or complex traffic flows, and help with data-based decision making.

The rapid availability of traffic speed data allows deep neural network methods to take advantage of the nonlinear properties of traffic speed data far more completely and to make great strides in forecasting performance, because deep learning works with massive quantities of real-time and historical traffic speed data together. Additionally, deep learning models have common features that mix data-driven techniques and have shown great success in several applications, resulting in the large-scale deployment for short-term traffic forecasting. (Li, Y., et al., 2021) The deep learning techniques provide opportunities to develop data-driven mathematical representations of real-world processes. These representations can provide predictions regarding the future state of the modelled process or automate some of the activities. For solving complex learning tasks, Deep learning methods offer substantial benefits for researchers, especially when managing immense, large, and highly dimensional data.

2.2.1 Methods of Machine Learning

Coello et al. (Eds.) (2024) have edited a book that provides a selection of papers from ADCIS 2023, emphasising progress in data-driven computing and intelligent systems. This book includes current research in critical areas involving intelligent transportation, machine learning, and computational methods. The application and advancement of machine learning techniques have skyrocketed in the past ten years, and many non-parametric models have also been employed to control traffic(Li & Park, 2023). Many studies have previously investigated short-term traffic forecasting using supervised learning techniques like the K-means clustering algorithm, Support Vector Regression (SVR), and the k-nearest neighbour algorithm (Zhang et al., 2021).

A straightforward mapping-to-cells method was used to produce a spatiotemporal traffic map of a highway network. To predict short-term traffic speeds, support vector machine models are used with spatiotemporal data. For instance, research was done using traffic speed and congestion data gathered from the London metropolitan area in the United Kingdom. Their study sought to assess the accuracy of the forecasts produced and examine how well machine learning techniques like the Grey System Model, Support Vector Regression, and the K-nearest neighbour algorithm performed for short-term traffic forecasting Machine learning approaches are widely used to solve short-term traffic forecasting issues and have demonstrated effectiveness in forecasting under a range of transportation demands and border conditions (Wu et al., 2022).

The majority of current research in traffic forecasting focuses primarily on solving short-range network-based problems, even though short-term traffic forecasting techniques are well-established. It is very challenging to gather high-quality data from every sensor point on a very large road network for traffic speed forecasting, which leads to issues with data collection. It usually takes a great deal more time, effort, money, and processing power to solve the problem of missing data during the data pre-processing stage. From a practical standpoint, large networks with thousands of links or complex modules with multiple sub-modules for each link can be difficult to tune, and it is not practical to gather high-quality data for every small link. It is impossible to calibrate a large model with multiple sub-models on each link in a ten-thousand-link network, which presents a significant challenge for applications that handle online and real-time data (Alekseeva et al., 2021). For instance, traffic operators should have a thorough understanding of traffic allocation and congestion management choices thanks to precise information on future traffic forecasts supplied by intelligent transportation systems. Short-term traffic speed forecasting is an essential and trustworthy tool for better traffic network management and upkeep (N et al., 2018).

Algorithms for supervised learning, including Support Vector Machines (SVM), Random Forests, k-Nearest Neighbours (KNN), and Decision Trees, have been used extensively (Liu et al., 2021). Labelled traffic datasets with characteristics like vehicle counts, lane occupancy, average speed, time of day, and weather are used to train these models (Valencia et al., 2024). Following training, the models can predict future traffic levels using fresh input data or categorise traffic states (such as low, moderate, or high congestion). Traffic conditions without predefined categories are also grouped using unsupervised techniques such as clustering. Clustering, for instance, can be used to distinguish between normal congestion and incidents or to spot odd traffic patterns. These insights are invaluable for traffic authorities looking to identify irregularities and take prompt action (Thakre et al. 2024).

2.2.2 Methods of Deep Learning

The state of traffic congestion forecasting has improved tremendously via deep learning applications, compared to the previous state involving either statistics or shallow machine learning, which required substantial feature engineering. Two aspects of deep learning allow it to successfully model sequential, high-dimensional, and complex data and predict traffic congestion. First, deep learning approaches leverage their ability to learn hierarchical representations of raw input data while endogenously learning essential data transformations to predict the future. Second, deep learning approaches take advantage of historical and real-time traffic speed data (Clark et al., 2020) while reducing the impact of noise. The availability of traffic speed data has increased rapidly with the advent of sophisticated automatic data capture devices, and deep learning approaches accommodate the nonlinear behaviours of traffic speed data reasonably well, and can ultimately improve forecasting traffic congestion.

Deep learning techniques represent the tools to create data-driven mathematical representations to characterise real-world processes, mostly by using data directly related to the response variable. Manibardo et al. (2020) found that deep learning advances forecasting urban mobility by being able to model the complexity of the data, and Muhammad et al. (2021) noted that deep learning demonstrated skill in using multimodal data, including GPS and video, for improved traffic predictions.

Ding et al. (2021) have summarised progress in video compression systems that employ deep neural networks (DNNs), outlining important methods and illustrating a few case studies. The research highlights the state of the art and contributions of DNNs in achieving better compression efficiency and visual fidelity in media content. Deep learning techniques identify complex, non-linear patterns from rich and heterogeneous datasets; therefore, deep learning techniques have grown in popularity in the field of traffic congestion prediction. Compared to traditional Statistics and Shallow Machine learning models, deep learning techniques are preferred because deep learning techniques automatically learn hierarchical feature representations and account for spatiotemporal dependencies, which are intrinsic to the overall traffic dynamics.

Recently, many deep learning frameworks have demonstrated significant value, including the Multilayer Perceptron (MLP), Convolutional Neural Networks (CNN), Recurrent Neural Networks (RNN), and Long Short-term Memory (LSTM) (Zhang et al., 2020; Yang, 2021; Zhao et al., 2017). For example, Zhao et al. (2017) proposed an LSTM-based deep learning model for short-term traffic flow forecasting, demonstrating strong potential for temporal learning capabilities. Likewise, Ke et al. (2017) demonstrated a spatio-temporal deep learning model in their study for short-term forecasting of ride-hailing demand, and demonstrated the power of deep learning to leverage both spatial and temporal dependencies to better model a transportation system.

For the forecasting of traffic speeds using deep learning, deep learning varies in approaches to how it could be used for forecasting. Two types of approaches include the individual deep learning approach and the hybrid deep learning approach (Chen et al., 2019). Individual deep learning approaches are all applied with a single remaining one, which only modifies a single simple input data deep learning technique into a model. A hybrid deep learning approach is applied, with many deep learning techniques applied to produce a hybrid model. A hybrid deep learning approach by combining several deep learning methods to produce a hybrid model (Xing et al, 2021; Zhou et al, 2022).

(NN et al., 2019) For traffic management and control applications, various neural network learning models are being used, including, but not limited to, Neural Networks (NN), Recurrent Neural Networks (RNN), and Artificial Neural Networks (ANN) models. A Long Short-Term Memory network (LSTM) is a Deep learning model that can effectively characterise time correlations and perform well on time series data (Abuelfadl et al., 2022). In one study, it was found that LSTM networks were more effective than traditional models such as Auto-regressive Integrated Moving Average (ARIMA) models and Statistically Adjusted Engineering (SAE) models for forecasting traffic speed. An example of how a deep LSTM network and post-production prediction models could predict peak-hour traffic to simulate representative traffic situations and incident patterns.

Basic LSTM networks do not leverage spatial properties of data very effectively, but LSTM is good at modelling data. The waterfall LSTM framework was developed to work around this limitation of LSTMs (Wang, T., et al., 2023). Assuming that the models can use spatiotemporal data to forecast traffic flows. To enhance the predictive performance, some researchers augment the visual LSTM with geographic variables to predict traffic activity. In addition to augmenting LSTM with geographic variables, a further evolution of the research is the construction of a traffic prediction framework called the spatiotemporal random effects (STRE) model (Wang, Y., et al., 2018). The STRE model allows for flexible representation of traffic behaviour and provides computational cost savings. Spatiotemporal data improves predictions of short-term traffic flows with an adapted neural predictor with Time time-optimized multi-layer perceptron (MLP) architecture.

LSTMs retain the long-term dependencies needed to effectively predict time-series traffic (Wang, Z., et al., 2020). Given the advantage of prior knowledge (i.e., based on historical data), LSTMs demonstrate effective forecasts of traffic conditions (including peaks and recurring congestion routes), which are highly correlated with their use in comparison studies with traditional approaches such as RNNs or ARIMA forecasting within long-term horizons of forecasting. When used as CNN-LSTM hybrid models, an LSTM combined with CNN produces a framework to model spatial and temporal aspects of the traffic scene. As a base model for traffic sequence analysis and congestion categorisation, CNN-LSTM represents a strong base model for visual analysis of traffic sequences in this feed-forward second stacking ensemble (Ashraf et al., 2021; Bibi et al., 2021).

MLP is a connected, fully-connected, feedforward neural network that was applied to predict traffic flow, speed, or congestion levels because of its potential flexibility in the prediction of many-dimensional data structures. MLP performs well with tabular structured features that represent traffic volume, signal timing, or weather conditions, despite completely lacking recognition of temporal awareness. Although MLP exists completely autonomously as a base learner in a stacking ensemble, it can model complicated non-linear, high-dimensional relationships that simple models could never.

Convolutional Neural Networks (CNNs) have been performing well in several image processing applications. Due to this level of success, research is now being used in a few traffic forecasting studies to study reasonable and meaningful spatial features (Jawale, M., et al., 2023). Another example of these variations from the basic CNN is a CNN model combined with the Long Short-term Memory model (Awan, A. A., et al., 2024). The CNN-LSTM model has been used to improve forecast tasks like traffic speed with more overall accuracy. The short-term Traffic Flow forecasting CNN-LSTM-based approach (CLTFP) uses a 1D CNN to develop volumetric spatial features, and then, in the second case, together with the temporal by LSTM. Furthermore, to build crowd flow prediction in the urban area defining a deep spatial-temporal residual network is defined.

In traffic management systems, the survival of individuals during declared emergency incidents is a very ambiguous and tough issue. Concerning this type of problem, the focus is on the adaptation of the implementation of a path recommendation service for paramedics in emergencies. In another paper, the configuration of regularised linear models, together with a recursive sequence of tanh layers, was developed to extract the spatial-temporal information and forecast traffic speed on a route. Using Convolution Neural Networks (CNN) and Long Short-Term Memory (LSTM), a hybrid model named CLM was developed, and a constructed CNN model was used to extract the features in the traffic speed on a daily and sometimes weekly basis at the target area, which extracted the spatiotemporal features based on traffic speed together with the output of CNN by LSTM layers.

CNN has been employed to derive spatial features, including applications to traffic databases that are either directly linked to images or video frames collected or compiled from footage derived from surveillance. CNN architectures should be well-suited for visual traffic datasets, as they offer the opportunity for the researcher to automatically identify features such as the number of lanes, volume of traffic, and the occupancy of various road spaces (C. Wang et al, 2025). There is evidence from work like Sun et al. (2020) that models can attain improved accuracy of congestion detection, a factor that can influence the predictive accuracy of models, dependent on the deployed algorithms, when utilising the CNN approaches. Sato and Hotta (2020) further demonstrated that CNN architectures could be adapted to capsule networks with improved aspects regarding preservation of spatial hierarchy and part-whole relationships. Capsule Networks have been successfully utilised in traffic domains. Dafrallah et al. (2019) applied Caps Nets for pedestrian direction prediction and compared the results to CNNs. Liu et al. (2020) also used Caps Nets for vehicular scene segmentation tasks, and Qiu and Zhao (2022) proposed an improved Caps Net model for traffic flow prediction; all highlight the promise of improving traffic analysis and prediction.

SVC is frequently included in hybrid ensemble architectures to leverage the generalizability and applicability of SVC, despite not being a deep learning model. SVC has been applied to segregate congestion classes with maximum margin, and is effective in spaces with high-dimensional feature sets, i.e., many features per sample. SVC provides a discriminative layer, which is useful in increasing the robustness of classification when incorporated into hybrid deep ensemble architectures, including CNNs, LSTMs, and MLPs. Therefore, ensembles with SVC produce better accuracy on edge cases as described by recent studies (Wang, T., et al. 2023) than classifiers that are neural-based.

Due to their respective merits, hybrid stacking approaches have been used in recent literature. SVC separates classes, MLP deals with complex feature acceptance, CNNs understand spatial features, and LSTM supports temporal dependencies. These properties are reflected in the hybrid stacking ensemble in this study, particularly the stacking where a Logistic Regression meta-learner takes the complementary perspectives from the base models of CNN-LSTM, MLP, and SVC. Empirical evidence shows that ensemble stacking outperforms the performance of base learners. For example, the ensemble CNN-LSTM-SVC achieved between 12 and 18% (Precision and Recall) improvement compared against all the single deep learning models on multiple datasets that contained urban traffic data (Rao et al., 2022).

2.3 Ensemble Learning Methods

To compare the performance of their congestion prediction using heterogeneous data sources, two different ensemble configurations have been used in this study (Qi, X., et al., 2020). The first model uses Support Vector Classifiers (SVC) and Multilayer Perceptrons (MLP) as base learners. A Logistic Regression meta-learner receives the predictions from these learners and uses them to determine the final congestion class. To produce out-of-fold predictions that stop data leakage and enhance generalisation, this model uses 5-fold cross-validation on structured, tabular traffic data. Traffic surveillance video spatiotemporal data is incorporated into the second ensemble model. The effect of temporal resolution has been evaluated using two video durations: 2-minute and 5-second clips. To identify important traffic elements, like cars and pedestrians, frames are taken out at predetermined intervals for both durations and processed using YOLOv8 object detection (Valencia et al., 2024; Liang et al., 2022). Weather information is added to the generated detections after the detections have been transformed into a CSV format.

Three base models are then trained using this engineered dataset: CNN-LSTM (for temporal dynamics capture), MLP (for pattern learning), and SVC (for decision boundary modelling). To compare the performance of the first model, the final prediction is once more made using logistic regression. Because ensemble learning techniques combine the outputs of several base models to increase accuracy, generalisation, and robustness, these techniques have drawn a lot of interest in traffic congestion prediction tasks. To forecast network traffic in VANETs, Ahmadi et al. (2023) suggest an ensemble-based machine learning framework. This framework improves prediction accuracy through the use of ensemble techniques, which integrate many algorithms to manage the varying nature of a vehicular network setting.

Chen et al. (2020) introduce a traffic-condition-aware ensemble learning model that acts as a decision maker for traffic flow prediction. The researchers' model approach dynamically adapts to varying traffic conditions, enhancing prediction accuracy and reliability. Ensemble approaches combine the strengths of various learners rather than depending on a single predictive algorithm, which improves performance, especially in complex and unpredictable environments like urban traffic networks. Boosting, stacking, and bagging are some of the most popular ensemble techniques. Every method uses a different approach to integrate base models and lower the error. The goal of bagging, also known as bootstrap aggregating, is to lower variance by training several models on various data subsets. Boosting train models to fix the mistakes of earlier models, one after the other, to lessen bias. Predictions from multiple base learners are combined and fed into a meta-learner to produce the final output, a process known as stacking or stacked generalisation.

Recent research has demonstrated that stacking outperforms other ensemble techniques in multi-class classification tasks like congestion level prediction. For instance, when tested on urban traffic datasets, stacking-based ensembles outperformed standalone SVM, Random Forest, or XGBoost models in terms of accuracy and F1 scores in a comparative study by Zhou et al. 2023. And Dong et al. (2021) present a novel ensemble reinforcement learning model combined with a gated recursive network for traffic speed forecasting. The proposed approach improves prediction accuracy by leveraging both ensemble learning and temporal dynamics.

2.3.1 Deep Ensemble Learning

To increase final prediction performance and provide better generalisation, ensemble learning models mix many base or individual models with various techniques. Furthermore, sophisticated, multi-layered deep learning models now perform better than conventional prediction models. Conversely, deep ensemble learning models combine the unique benefits of these two models to create a more successful prediction model. Only a small percentage of the numerous models created for traffic flow prediction in the literature are based on ensemble learning. However, because ensemble learning-based models are built by merging either individual models generated using different combinations of the same method or individual models developed using distinct methods, the researchers offer improved accuracy and generalizability. For traffic flow forecasting, combining several models in this manner can improve the final forecasting accuracy while avoiding overfitting. Because each model only addresses one component of the final model, the final model achieves a higher prediction accuracy and offers a more comprehensive representation than individual models. Present a unique deep ensemble model for traffic flow prediction, concentrating on ensemble learning techniques (Cini and Aydin, 2024). The following is Equation 3, the formula for an ensemble model:

$$F(t) = \sum_{i=1}^{N} \beta_i \cdot h_i(t) \tag{3}$$

Where $F(t)$, represents the final model prediction at time t. $h_i(t)$ denotes the prediction of ith base model, β_i Is the weight of the ith individual model, and $N$is the total number of individual models in the ensemble.

The ensemble learning model assigns weight to each model based on this formula. For this reason, giving each model equal weight is the most popular strategy in the literature. One problem with this strategy is that, without taking into account the prediction performance of individual models, each model contributes equally to the final prediction. The performance of the ensemble model is limited when a fixed weight is assigned to each model because this reduces the model's capacity for generalisation. Therefore, in this study, a flexible and robust Stack ensemble model is presented to increase the prediction accuracy. The weights are assigned by the suggested model according to the performance of each model and the change in traffic conditions.

2.3.2 CNN-LSTM, MLP, and SVC in an Ensemble Model

For more contextual congestion prediction, the second ensemble combines environmental features and video analytics. To determine the number and kind of vehicles, the pipeline first extracts frames from traffic videos and then looks for objects. A feature-rich dataset is created by combining these outputs with meteorological data (temperature, humidity, and visibility). This pipeline's base models consist of CNN-LSTM, which uses sequential image data to identify spatiotemporal patterns, and the engineered feature set is processed by the MLPClassifier. Strong classification capabilities on structured inputs are contributed by the SVC (Li et al., 2020).

Cao et al. (2020) proposed a hybrid model based on the CNN-LSTM that effectively captures both space and time features in a singular model to predict traffic speed accurately. This model outperforms certain traditional methods in dynamic traffic scenarios. Bilotta et al. (2022) present a short-term city traffic flow prediction model using convolutional deep learning techniques. The model approach accurately captures spatial-temporal traffic patterns, yielding a better prediction accuracy of traffic flow in urban settings (Peng, H. et al., 2020). And Bogaerts et al. (2020) propose a Graph CNN-LSTM neural network model for both short- and long-term traffic forecasting using vehicle trajectory data. The CNN approach effectively captures spatial and temporal dependencies, improving the accuracy of traffic predictions. Dai et al. (2019) suggest a short-term traffic flow prediction method on urban roads using the ideas of space-time analysis and GRU networks. The model was able to capture temporal patterns effectively and thus improved the accuracy of traffic prediction. Ma et al. (2021) implemented capsule networks with nested LSTM memory models to predict the speed of transportation networks.

The Logistic Regression meta-learner then combines the predictions of the is an ensemble of models are put together, and it makes a final classification of congestion. These ensemble methods work in real-world systems. For instance, demonstrated that ensemble methods, stacking models with classifiers such as Random Forest and Support Vector Machines, and using Logistic Regression as a meta-learner, provide tremendous benefit over single models' classification on a congestion prediction based on accuracy (Saleem et al. 2022). The authors provide a valuable illustration of the advantage of multi-model architectures, as the detected model can detect more complex traffic patterns from many dimensions rather than using a single, one-dimensional model.

Ensemble models provide a methodical way to balance bias and variance while utilising the variety of underlying algorithms, as opposed to individual deep learning or machine learning models. In urban traffic research, empirical results consistently show that stacking methods are more robust to overfitting, better handle missing or noisy data, and generate more interpretable and flexible predictions in a range of temporal and spatial contexts (Li et al., 2023). Both structured data-based and video-driven ensemble configurations are reflected in the two models this study presents, which are in line with current developments in intelligent traffic monitoring systems. In intelligent transportation environments, the design seeks to support real-time traffic decision-making in addition to increasing prediction accuracy.

Support Vector Classifier (SVC) and Multilayer Perceptron (MLP Classifier) are chosen as base learners in the initial stacking configuration utilised in this investigation. (Ahmadi et al., 2023) The SVC focuses on optimising class separability with robust generalisation, particularly in the presence of sparse training data, whereas the MLP Classifier captures intricate nonlinear relationships across high-dimensional traffic features. Logistic Regression is employed as the meta-learner to successfully integrate these learners. Each base learner produces out-of-fold predictions as part of the stacking process, which uses a 5-fold cross-validation strategy during training.

The logistic regression model is then trained using these predictions as input features. The meta-learner, at inference time, decides the final congestion class (low, medium, or high) of a new data row by aggregating the real-time predictions made by the base models. A meta-learner structure will facilitate more stable generalisation and enhance detection capabilities along class boundaries. It is polyfunctional and is more accurate than flat architectures, such as either a single MLP or SVC model, when dealing with noisy or imbalanced traffic datasets (Rasaizadi et al., 2022).

2.4 Object Detection in Traffic Systems

As object detection can detect and classify vehicles, pedestrians, and other road-based objects in real-time, it has become an important part of intelligent traffic management systems that provide necessary information one stage before other processes that will be used for adaptive signal control, congestion prediction, and the assessment of traffic flows. Chen et al. (2023) introduced a zone-based clustering method for pedestrian group detection and tracking. The approach considers spatial zones and group dynamics to improve accuracy and robustness when there are more complex environments. There has been a rapid increase in scalability and granularity, and in this time, the disproportionate success of deep learning-based vision approaches, mostly detectors based on convolutional neural networks (CNNs), which have been shown to outperform traditional methods based on various types of sensors. Wayfinding using these techniques with object detection is a major aspect of traffic systems when it comes to observing and managing vehicle flow. The use of an adaptive video-based system utilising background subtraction and object classification techniques on video streams to collect real-time traffic data. Benchmark datasets like the UCI traffic dataset are useful and dependable for traffic data that supports model development (Dua & Graff, 2019) when evaluating and training such systems.

The adaptive video system tracks vehicles visible in the video frame. This is relevant because the system can indicate how many vehicles there are, and also estimate speed based on video recording frames (Chang et al., 2019). In addition, cooperative vehicle-infrastructure systems have been put to use to detect accidents in real-time through vehicle and roadside unit communication, which would improve detection time and situational awareness (Tian et al., 2019). The authors use several methods, including MOG2 (for the background subtraction) and OpenCV, that provide tracking ability of vehicles and allow reliable classification with uncertainty in dynamic environments. Bouraffa et al. (2024) examine traffic event detection using space-filling curves, making comparisons between optical flow and deep learning-based techniques, and focus on computational efficiency while still obtaining reliable detection performance for intelligent transportation systems.

Real-time traffic situations have experienced cutting-edge accuracy from modern object detection systems such as YOLO (You Only Look Once), SSD (Single Shot MultiBox Detector), and Faster R-CNN (Zhu, J., et al., 2019; Zhou et al., 2022). YOLOv8 has rapidly become the top traffic detection algorithm because it can balance accuracy and detection speed across multiple environmental features, such as lighting and other environmental aspects. Reported that YOLOv8 can significantly support further facilitation of resource allocation, make vehicle detection from visualisation better, and improve traffic management of metropolitan regions. It outperformed previous models such as Faster R-CNN by reducing false detection rates at urban intersections. Reducing false detections at intersections is invaluable for real-time traffic analysis and control because it means reduced accidents and improved roadway safety (Zuraimi & Zaman, 2021). And utilising a deep learning approach that employs Faster R-CNN, Chaudhuri (2024) defined an intelligent traffic management scheme that utilises vehicle Detection and Classification. The methodological approach of the model enhanced real-time data, monitoring, and decision-making tasks in complex urban situations. Hu and colleagues (2019) developed a scale-insensitive CNN model to assist in the rapid detection of vehicles in traffic systems.

Two comparative video-based prediction pipelines in the current study rely heavily on object detection. In the first method, YOLOv8 is directly applied to every frame of 2-minute video clips to identify objects like cars, trucks, bikes, and pedestrians. A structured detection_results.csv file contains the detection results, which include the bounding box coordinates, object type, frame index, and confidence score. This approach gives congestion analysis a wider temporal context. In contrast, the second approach focuses on 5-second video clips, which are first decomposed into individual frames at 1-second intervals. Object detection is then applied to these shorter segments, allowing for a more fine-grained temporal resolution and quicker processing cycles.

Both methods contribute to independent pipelines for feature extraction, integration of weather data, and training base models, and the detected objects in each frame are stored in the same way (Tsalikidis, N., et al. 2024). The rationale of the dual-clip approach was to evaluate how the length of the video clip impacted the responsiveness of the model and prediction performances. Shorter clips (5-second) facilitate near real-time assessment and are therefore more applicable to adaptive traffic control and rapid detection, whilst long clips (2-minute) provide comprehensive perspectives on traffic flow evolution. Current comparative literature, such as Liu et al. 2024, has concluded that temporal granularity greatly influences model performance in all contested circumstances with traffic variability.

Both detection pipelines' outputs (CSV logs and frame datasets) are used to train the base learners (CNN-LSTM, MLP, and SVC) in the second stacking ensemble model. These outputs also form the foundation for sophisticated feature extraction. Congestion level classification is made possible by this configuration, which also offers a scalable framework for incorporating contextual data like weather conditions, the time of day, and traffic patterns. The advantages of vision-based object detection over conventional traffic sensors include portability, contextual scene understanding, and multi-class detection (Huang et al., 2020). Traditional systems like infrared counters and loop detectors frequently have installation limitations and lack object-level granularity. When compared to hardware-based solutions, computer vision models increased classification accuracy in complex traffic environments by more than 20%. Object detection improves detection accuracy and allows for dynamic model designs that can adjust to various temporal scopes when incorporated into traffic prediction systems. This development makes it possible to make decisions about traffic control and urban mobility planning more intelligently, quickly, and precisely.

2.5 Related Works

(Cini et al., 2024) Take a deep ensemble approach to long-term traffic flow prediction by integrating advanced neural network models, where these develop a method by leveraging the benefits of several different temporal and spatial deep learning models to improve prediction performance. The method makes use of structured sensor-based datasets, such as the California PeMS, that represent historical data of traffic flow, speed, and occupancy, to train the model. Despite demonstrating high accuracy in predicting traffic behaviours for extended periods, this framework is limited to use in situations of established sensor infrastructures. In addition, the study excludes real-time situational contexts that are often critical to fairly prompt decisions in scenarios of unanticipated congestion, such as situational or visual road conditions or external environmental contexts.

Research further builds and expands on this work by developing a multimodal stacking ensemble model using structured data as well as unstructured video inputs. Whereas Cini et al. (2024) only utilised numerical time-series data, this approach uses video-based object detection using YOLOv8 to produce features such as vehicle type, count, and bounding box measurements from short video clips. These structured visual features are enriched with real weather data (temperature, humidity, and weather conditions) to provide the model with additional context. This combined input is analysed through a deep learning ensemble of CNN-LSTM, MLP, and SVC models with the use of logistic regression as a meta-learner. By merging visual assessment of scenes with structured, sensor-like inputs, the gaps left by Cini and Aydin (2024) and a multi-modal, adaptive approach for traffic congestion prediction across a variety of real-world settings are proposed.

L. Qu et al. (2019) offer a method for long-term daily traffic flow forecasting that utilises a DNN model. Their approach emphasises the importance of historical traffic flow to inform the deep learning model, which measures more involved, various temporal patterns over longer aggregations of time. This study achieves this with structured numerical data (i.e., sensors or loop detectors), but ultimately, their method seeks to model long-term traffic trends, does not estimate real-time impacts, add perceived visual trends, nor consider environmental and other variations that impact traffic. The main advantage of their model is that it learns long-term influences in traffic when estimating long-term flows with solely historical data, for long periods, and in reasonably stable traffic situations.

Whereas L. Qu et al. (2019) build on this knowledge base with only a longitudinal component, this research builds on it by adding additional variables to the prediction process. L. Qu et al. (2019) utilise just time-series data; therefore, this study doesn't use the direct relationship found in video frame features obtained via object detection (vehicle count, vehicle type, etc.) as well as contextual weather data to help predict future traffic congestion. The outcome is a more stable ensemble model that is responsive to changes to traffic, weather, and time. The addition of visual and environmental factors in the present stacking ensemble expands the data-driven neural network perspective (such as L. Qu's) and ought to create a more comprehensive method for modelling traffic congestion.

Khalil et al. (2024) comprehensively reviewed advanced learning technologies utilised in Intelligent Transportation Systems (ITS). The researchers described these technologies that promise a lot but also come with challenges. The authors detail an array of machine and deep learning methods and how these adapt to enhance timely decision-making and improve real-time adaptive traffic control and predictive analysis. The analysis noted the importance of combining various sources of data - sensor data, vehicular networks, and even environmental data - which will aid in improving the robustness and accuracy of ITS applications. The authors also discussed limitations such as scalability issues, computation requirements, and the need for context-aware models.

This wider view reinforces the authority argued for in this present research, which adapts to the stated conditions by building on multiple learning models and data sources in a stacking ensemble method, instead of following the example of the single model methods tested in Khalil et al. (2024), and is combining not just one type of visual data (through object detection in traffic video) with each of the environmental features, but is creating a model to predict traffic congestion that is much more adaptable to location and situation. Khalil et al.'s research illustrates a wider acceptance for multi-modal learning, including the need for model interpretability (which the predictive framework was designed to embody). Therefore, it strengthens the conceptual rationale for utilising ensemble learning as a development pathway in the realm of modern ITS research.

Ganesan et al. (2024) present a thorough review of these deep learning-based motion planning and end-to-end learning methods for the self-driving domain. The paper discusses the theoretical possibilities of deep learning models capable of planning and controlling vehicle movements, autonomous integration of perception, decision making, and control functionality in an end-to-end approach. The review also navigates through several methods, including reinforcement learning, imitation learning, and neural networks, that have resulted in advances in the autonomous driving domain. In particular, the review draws attention to the end-to-end learning approach, introducing the model learning to map sensor information into driving actions (without explicit rules based on "a priori" systems).

Their focus is on the navigation of an autonomous vehicle (Lee et al., 2020). There are strong similarities in their use of deep learning and the current research in traffic flow prediction, particularly when it comes to decision-making in real-time (Aldakkhelallah & Simic, 2021; Muhammad et al., 2021). This finding's contribution, the merging of visual and environmental data into a predictive model for traffic congestion, is similar in spirit to (Ganesan et al. 2024; Kliestik et al., 2022). Both works utilise deep learning to drive decisions based on sensory inputs, although the present study uses it to predict traffic conditions, while those studies use it to control the vehicle. With the ability to utilise multiple inputs such as video and weather data, the objective of the present research was to apply deep learning to create a real-time prediction specifically in the dynamic area of traffic, complementing the motion planning models used in autonomous driving.

(Falaschetti et al. 2024) Proposed an efficient embedded real-time system for detecting vehicles and pedestrians using compressed Tiny YOLO v3. The authors intend to advance the computational efficiency of object detection models to deploy to embedded systems with limited resources. This study optimised the YOLO v3 architecture and accomplished real-time vehicle and pedestrian detection, especially important for intelligent transportation systems that act according to changing traffic conditions in an immediate time frame. The study addresses the trade-offs between model size, detection precision, and processing speed, while advocating for the use of lightweight models in practice.

This work gives a valuable context for the implementation of real-time object detection in the area of transportation. While Falaschetti et al. 2024 focus on embedded systems to detect vehicles and pedestrians, the present study builds upon the concept of visual data processing by extending capabilities to predict traffic congestion. Rather than limiting the scope to object detection, this approach integrates object detection outcomes with weather and other environmental data to predict congestion. Using a compressed object detection model, as presented in Falaschetti et al.'s (2024), is consistent with the focus on processing efficiency found in this research, as the developed ensemble framework is also intended to process large quantities of information that require real-time information processing with high prediction accuracy.

Adl et al. (2024) present an intelligent vision-based framework for counting vehicle movements at intersections. The authors use a fisheye camera system and a self-learning mechanism for a wide-angle view of the complex environment at the intersection, and adaptive learning improves detection and tracking accuracy over time for future uses. The authors state that their framework is autonomous, and it can refine its performance without manual retuning; thus, it can be suited for variable urban conditions, which regularly change upon each use.

While the main goal is distinguishable from predicting traffic to count vehicles, this study also offers good methodologies that can be useful in the present study. Both their use of real-time video analysis and adaptive learning systems shows a similar goal of extracting useful transportation-related patterns from visual data. On the other hand, while their real-time vehicle monitoring system is fixed to the roadway, this study compiles video clips that help extract object-level features while considering relevant contextual information to predict congestion. Their advanced vehicle-detection systems further support the application of vision systems in transportation analytics. The findings also validate video input as a sound basis for predictive modelling.

While the advancement of work by Adl et al. (2024) is a significant step towards detecting and counting vehicles at crossings by employing fisheye camera technologies and self-learning algorithms, akin to this work, Adl et al. (2024) do not approach forecasting future traffic conditions. Their system is engineered for detection and accurate object tracking in real time, with no predictive capabilities to determine probable future congestion based on the movements detected. This is a meaningful gap in research, particularly when data will be employed in future applications for active traffic coordination.

This research acknowledges and fills this gap by developing an extension of video-based vehicle detection aimed at also predicting using an amalgamation of object-level traffic characteristics contextualised together with other information, such as weather. The contribution is that this framework is not seeking just to observe congestion but rather to provide a more comprehensive solution aimed at predicting and managing traffic into the future.

Yıldız et al. (2023) proposed a new ensemble learning model that is referred to as HIICNN (Hybrid Image Improving and CNN), which aids in the complete recognition task of assigned tasks before receiving the final prediction from the CNN based on the combined image enhancement and spoiling images. HIICNN combines image enhancement and occlusion or review, which is an important step in many domains of interest. The task-dependent qualities of this framework call on differing image enhancement techniques, multiple CNN implementations, and a meta-learner component where the predictions of multiple CNNs are combined into one final meta-learner prediction. Yıldiz et al. (2023) emphasise that ensemble methods are well-suited for tasks with noise, varying illumination, and level of image quality, which are regarded as some of the most degrading elements a recognition system will encounter when dealing with visual input in the real-world transportation scene.

The HIICNN framework has been shown to have impressive performance in static image classification, especially for traffic signs. However, it does not address traffic flow prediction or dynamic video data. This is a key gap in the research undertaken to assist real-time traffic management, which increasingly demands predictive systems capable of utilising both the visual and contextual information from video streams. This research does not use the term ensemble learning; however, it uses some form of ensemble learning to shift the use of features derived from video and environmental data to forecast traffic congestion through a multi-model construct. In contrast to Yıldiz et al. (2023), which shows classification accuracy of static objects, the research applies stacking to a new temporal and predictive domain that is focused on real-world traffic behaviour modelling.

Valencia et al. (2024) explored the impact of various preprocessing techniques on the accuracy of a vehicle counting system based on the YOLO algorithm (you only look once). All of the testing for their work was completed for offline video analysis, and the researchers analysed how factors such as frame resolution, illumination, and background subtraction affected YOLO's ability to identify and count several vehicles. The authors also state that tuning the preprocessing stage increases the number of correct detections and the reliability of automated vehicle monitoring systems in traffic videos.

Although pre-processing effects have been thoroughly examined, this study's scope is still restricted to offline counting and does not examine predictive applications. This indicates a glaring research need, particularly in situations where managing traffic requires foreseeing future conditions. The idea of frame-level pre-processing and detection is expanded upon in this work, but it moves closer to a dynamic congestion prediction framework. The present model shifts the focus from static analysis to real-time predictive modelling by combining object detection outputs with contextual information like weather and time of day. Then, it uses those enriched features in a stacking ensemble to forecast traffic congestion levels.

Chaudhuri (2024) puts forward a smart traffic management method based on Faster R-CNN, a region-based convolutional neural network (CNN) for real-time vehicle detection and tracking. The method's purpose is to capture the traffic flow through the feeds of surveillance camera video, with the consideration of vehicle localisation and counting to understand congestion status. Chaudhuri's paper demonstrated that Faster R-CNN allows for high-precision vehicle detection in complex and high-density traffic situations. Moreover, the model is used in a real-time pipeline that provides urban traffic management based on high-accuracy situational awareness.

While the effectiveness of the Faster R-CNN-based system for object detection is noteworthy, the study does not extend its research into the realm of traffic predictive capabilities. The study is situated in a "now" state (monitoring) and lacks predictive capabilities for traffic congestion. This is a gap, and monitoring cannot facilitate an active role in managing traffic disruption through real-time detection algorithms alone. The present research will fill the absence of predictive capabilities and recognise the value of expanding the use of video-based vehicle detection as predictive, by directly utilising the output of detection models (that utilise YOLO as an example) with additional contextual and temporal components, including local historical patterns and integrating them with stacking ensembles to forecast future levels of detected congestion. The addition of predictive and forecasting considerations is a development in traffic management capabilities because it allows the timely development of proactive decisions with a more intelligent transport system.

Zheng et al. (2022) introduced a hybrid deep learning model, GCN-GAN, that combines Graph Convolutional Networks (GCNs) with Generative Adversarial Networks (GANs) for use in traffic flow prediction. In this model, GCNs model the spatial dependencies between the traffic sensors represented as a road network graph, and GANs, encapsulated with LSTM within the generator, model temporal dynamics by learning realistic flows of traffic.

This approach was validated using the METR-LA dataset, which contains speed data from 207 loop detectors on the highways of Los Angeles, all recorded at 5-minute intervals. The results of this experiment demonstrate that GCN-GAN outperforms traditional statistical and deep learning methods like ARIMA, SVR, and DCRNN, and deep learning layered models like LSTM, especially during times of severe congestion.

While GCN-GAN is a promising model, there are limitations to the study. The model relies only on loop detector data; it does not integrate multimodal sources such as video, weather, or GPS data that can enrich models and are essential for practical applications. Also, the spatial graph is static and pre-defined based on physical sensor locations. While decent representation of distances on a map, this static graph does not represent the dynamic urban traffic systems that the graph intends to observe.

The model was confined to the METR-LA dataset for observation and evaluation, limiting applicability and generalizability to other cities or conditions. Finally, the model, like many deep learning approaches, is non-interpretable, reducing the model's utility as important historical information is lost while justifying predictions in intelligent transportation systems.

2.6 Summary of Gaps Identified

Several research projects in intelligent transportation systems have tackled the issues of vehicle detection, traffic prediction, and traffic behaviour with a variety of deep learning algorithms and many limitations following the solitary use of vehicle detection for prediction or by failing to integrate real-time data context. Table 1 summarises 25 significant past works and provides a diversity of approaches while directing attention to some practical limitations that will inform the current research. While important strides have been made, a common framework linking spatial-temporal features, object-level context, and environmental context remains to be fully explored. This uses cases identified in the previous sections to address those gaps by proposing an ensemble-based video-centric model leveraging USB and contextual data in real time.

Table 1: Summary of Gaps Identified in Traffic Prediction Models

S. No.	Author(s) & Year	Dataset/Data Used	Model/Method Used	Limitation
1	Cini et al., 2024	Traffic Flow Data	Deep Ensemble Learning	Constrained by availability, large levels of data, and computational complexity.
2	Qu, L., et al. (2019)	Daily Traffic Data	Deep Neural Network	Model performance is compromised by daily traffic variability.
3	Khalil, R. A., et al. (2024)	Traffic Data & Environmental Sensors	Advanced Learning Technologies	Lack of adaptation in real-time based on normal traffic conditions.
4	Ganesan, M., et al. (2024)	Motion Planning & Vehicle Data	Deep Learning for Autonomous Vehicles	Only self-driving application scenarios are restricted during real-world traffic.
5	Falaschetti, L., et al. (2024)	Vehicle & Pedestrian Detection Data	Tiny YOLO v3	High computational resource requirements inhibit scalability.
6	Adl, M., et al. (2024)	Fisheye Camera System Data	Self-learning System	Only for counting vehicles at intersections.
7	Chaudhuri, A.	Vehicle Data	Faster R-CNN	Limitations on

	(2024)			generalizability in all diverse traffic conditions.
8	Tsalikidis, N., et al. (2024)	Traffic & Weather Data	Multi-step Approach	Requires multiple and diverse data compilations, which may not be present each time.
9	Lana, I., et al. (2018)	Traffic Flow Data	Traffic Forecasting Models	Lacks consideration of long-term changes in traffic.
10	Wang, Z., et al. (2020)	Traffic Flow Data	LSTM Encoder-Decoder	Too computationally expensive for long-term predictions.
11	Zhang, D., & Kabuka, M. R. (2018)	Weather Condition & Traffic Data	GRU-based Deep Learning	Does not perform well during extreme weather conditions
12	Bogaerts, T., et al. (2020)	Trajectory Data	Graph CNN-LSTM	Only applicable to short-term prediction for traffic.
13	Li, Y., et al. (2021)	Long-term Traffic Flow Data	Hybrid Deep Learning Framework	Fail to adapt to real-time traffic changes.
14	Liu, X., et al. (2024)	Traffic Data	Improved YOLOv8	Only capable of limited scalability of mobility in traffic environments.
15	Mystakidis, A., et al. (2025)	Traffic Data	Emerging Techniques for Traffic Prediction	Did not benchmark extensively against existing models.
16	Liu, J., et al. (2020)	Traffic Flow Data	Ensemble Approach (Deep Belief Networks)	Difficulty in capturing long-term trends in traffic data.
17	Awan, A. A., et al. (2024)	Traffic Speed Data	Deep Stacking-based Ensemble	Limitations of data quality/accuracy of speed data.
18	Chen, Y., et al. (2020)	Traffic & Weather Data	Ensemble Learning	Lacks real-time functionality with daily traffic variations.
19	Lim, X. R., et al. (2023)	Traffic Sign Recognition Data	Ensemble Learning for Sign	The only limitation of sign recognition is not for larger traffic flow

			Recognition	prediction.
20	Bilotta, S., et al. (2022)	City Traffic Flow Data	Convolutional Deep Learning	Does not take into account real traffic variability.
21	Shabbir, A., et al. (2024)	Acoustic Vehicle Detection Data	Stacking-based Ensemble Deep Learning	Limitations of focus can be different urban environments.
22	Rane, N., et al. (2024)	General Traffic & Machine Learning Data	Ensemble & Machine Learning Techniques	Focused on high-level terms rather than improvements in traffic specifics.
23	Liu, R., & Shin, S. Y. (2025)	Traffic Data	Traffic Flow Prediction Methods	Failure to compare their parameters of performance against modern ensemble techniques.
24	Zheng, M., et al. (2019)	Traffic Accident Data	CNN-based Deep Learning	Focus only on accident severity rather than general traffic prediction.
25	Yildiz, G., et al. (2023)	Traffic Sign Data	Hybrid Image & CNN Stacking Ensemble	Only for traffic sign recognition.

The studies presented in the table explore various methods and datasets used for traffic congestion prediction and management. Compare multiple machine learning algorithms for traffic prediction, highlighting the lack of real-world testing. (Sahu et al. 2024) Focus on a low-cost real-time traffic system using modified YOLOv8 and GWO-LSTM for edge deployment, but their solution may not be suitable for complex areas. Huang et al. (2018) integrate weather data into traffic flow predictions using a GRU-based model, though the performance can suffer from incomplete weather data. Sun, B., et al. (2020) review traffic congestion prediction based on spatiotemporal data, though their model lacks real-time feedback.

The World Health Organisation (2016) assesses the impact of ambient air pollution on health, but its study is not directly related to traffic congestion. Provide an overview of emerging techniques in traffic congestion prediction, focusing on innovations without detailed implementation. Ding et al. (2025) discuss the impact of urban planning on traffic congestion through nonlinear analysis, but their model doesn't address real-time management. Finally,

Wang et al. (2025) focus on traffic congestion recognition using convolutional neural networks across different traffic scenarios, but their approach is limited to specific conditions. These studies highlight the diversity in methodologies, data sources, and limitations across traffic congestion research, pointing to the need for more generalised, real-time solutions for urban traffic management.

The literature review table presents a thorough review of recent developments and advances in traffic prediction models, predictive data sources, and methodologies. The review table emphasises the heterogeneity of datasets used, ranging from traffic flow and environmental sensor data sets to fish-eye cameras and acoustic inputs. There are also various machine learning and deep learning methods used, such as Deep Neural Networks (DNNs), GRU, LSTM Encoder-Decoder, Graph CNN-LSTM, various YOLO approaches, and ensemble learning methods (Rangari, A. P. et al., 2022).

Also common to the review are limitations concerning scalability, difficulty adapting and responding to real-time and long-term changes in traffic, inhibitory computational demands, and limited generalizability to varied traffic environments. Also, several models are highly specific in scope, mostly concentrating on narrow approaches such as counting vehicles, sign recognition, and other self-driving applications, thus limiting their applicability regarding overall traffic congestion prediction and backward design. Shabbir et al. (2024) introduced a smart city traffic management system using acoustic signals for vehicle detection. Shabbir et al. employed a stacking-based ensemble deep learning model that combines multiple learners to achieve better detection performance. The study shows, for the first time, that using acoustic data is an effective input format for intelligent traffic investigation and analysis in complex urban settings.

Although there are limitations, it is clear that adopting an ensemble deep learning model when combined with CNN-LSTM, MLP, and SVC is justified. This hybridised structure is advantageous in that it takes advantage of the strengths of each model. CNN-LSTM captures spatial-temporal sequences from video data efficiently (NN, L. et al., 2019). MLP excels at utilising high-dimensional features from structured datasets, while neglecting input features with unknown boundaries. In contrast, SVC performs its best in classification based on congestion levels obtained with structured predictive data boundaries.

The ensemble learning structure is viable because it can directly address the model weaknesses that arise from using a solitary model. For instance, using multiple models allows for having multiple perspectives regarding what is learned from using each unique outcome as it relates to improved prediction precision or accuracy, adaptability, and generalizability in traffic environments. Happy to note that ensemble deep learning style models resonate within current research gaps noted in the literature review table, such as the need for models that adapt to real-time situations, that employ holistic approaches to traffic understanding or congestion prediction, and that can utilise multiple input modalities, which particularly give them a strong opportunity for practical application in complex urban contexts.

2.7 Summary

Chapter Two of this thesis offers an organised review of current traffic congestion analysis literature, predictive approaches for forecasting, and advanced machine learning methods for traffic congestion. The chapter starts with a discussion on the causes and consequences of traffic congestion, demonstrating issues related to urbanisation and demand, and the limited road network and heterogeneous traffic conditions in the expanding, developing region and/or country. Next is a review of traditional approaches to measuring and forecasting congestion, including statistical models and early predictive models.

This is followed by a review of machine learning and deep learning techniques, providing an overview of the different approaches while reviewing the strengths and weaknesses of the learner approaches regarding Deep Neural Networks (DNN), Gated Recurrent Units (GRU), Long Short-term Memory (LSTM) based encoders, etc. The review will also provide some detail on ensemble learning, where single models like CNN-LSTM, Multi-layer Perceptron (MLP), and Support Vector Classification (SVC) are more capable collectively, functioning in three areas of feature extraction, non-linear classification, and non-trivial assumptions to make useful models to generalise across various types of data.

The review will also present recent works on methods and models, with clear comparisons, alongside the variety of datasets, input modes, and architectures. This will reveal the limitations of current works that restrict scalability, real-time dynamics, and narrow categories, such as vehicle count or sign recognition. New techniques, including object detection techniques based on the YOLO methods, and traffic-aware models that include weather or audio data, offer a new direction, but mostly have no generalizable objectives to model for deployable traffic detection or prediction capacity.

Those studies with an ensemble framework, such as Shabbir et al. (2024), employed stacking and demonstrated the promise of stacking models into a more complete developed area of study as opposed to the partial or specific focus on a learning task regarding traffic classification. The review of literature in this chapter identified a gap in the research, as there are currently no generalised, real-time, multi-modal systems for measuring and predicting traffic congestion. This supports the use of ensemble deep learning, designed to capitalise on the methodical strengths of CNN-LSTM, MLP, and SVC while also providing a route to modelling the depth of complexity captured understandably regarding traffic research context (vehicular, human, socio-technical, and urban planning), reflecting the rapidly developing areas/countries with high urbanisation and consequential pressures placed on congestion.

Chapter 3: Research Methodology

This chapter discusses the systematic process implemented to undertake this research into traffic congestion prediction using an ensemble deep learning framework. Having a clear and methodical approach is fundamental for accurately, reliably, and reproducibly achieving the research aims. The methodology was both qualitative and quantitative, involving video-based data extraction, feature engineering, deep learning modelling, and performance comparison. The study emphasised a method driven by the research problem, whereby appropriate procedures (step-by-step, i.e., from data collection to model validation) were undertaken to enhance the predictive capability.

The chapter commenced with the overall design of the research, describing aspects of the data collection process (video traffic images and associated environmental conditions). The next sections explain how the raw data is processed and how the data is converted into features for model training. The main body of the chapter then described and presented the ensemble deep learning model developed, plus the traditional comparison models. It also discusses the evaluation metrics that were used for performance analysis and lists the tools and technologies that were used in the implementation. Collectively, these aspects would provide a very strong methodological basis for the study.

3.1 Data Set Description

In many studies within the domain of traffic congestion research, public datasets are commonly employed. These datasets are typically derived from public repositories like Kaggle and other open-source networks. However, this research aimed to take a more contextualised approach by using real-world recorded video data from urban intersections. While public datasets can be beneficial for exploratory studies, this study can also suffer from a lack of specificity, environmental variability, or complexities, and often, specific time zones of reference may be absent in real-world situations that happened in complex urban contexts like a real day. To fill the gap, video data was collected in real time under the auspices of the Bengaluru Traffic Management System.

A formal data request through a written proposal to the Bengaluru Traffic Police Department, which granted permissions to collect video data from various traffic intersections, from not one but a series of surveillance live video feeds across the city. The received video data was in Advanced Systems Format (.asf), which is a file format developed by Microsoft that provides efficient storage and optimised streaming. It enables synchronisation of video data along with audio and metadata. Video data in a surveillance environment often has to balance video quality and file size, so .asf is well-suited for these environments. For context, one day's worth of video recording data required approximately 15 GB of storage space, providing high-quality resolution video data over a longer period for experimental purposes. As an official acknowledgement email from the Bengaluru traffic police, confirmation that the data provision for 3rd,4th, and 5th October 2023 is included in Appendix A, while the dataset creation environment and implementation script are included in Appendix B.

Figure 2: Sample Photos Taken from Live Traffic Monitoring Videos

Figure 2 shows a screenshot from the real-time video surveillance footage received from the researcher, depicting the traffic conditions at Habbal Flyover. This is a screenshot from the video data used in the model. This screenshot represents a real-time traffic situation. The approach is used in each phase of the model for frame extraction, object detection, and congestion prediction (Feng et al., 2021).

In the present study, the original raw video data were pre-processed by converting the .asf format to the standard .mp4 format in 2-minute segments, as 2 minutes allow for the viewing of traffic patterns during both peak (i.e., congested) and non-peak times. Each video segment averaged around 11 MB in size, and the number of frames extracted from the 2-minute video segments can be variable based on the frame rate and encoding quality. Some video segments yielded around 313 frames, while others resulted in slightly higher or lower numbers. Short segments were selected due to system considerations because longer videos could have exceeded processing capabilities. Utilising short 2-minute video clips helped to keep the computational load limited and enabled us to focus on analysing traffic behavioural patterns located at particular intersections without overloading the processing capacity of the computer.

This section presents a detailed process for data collection to learn about traffic congestion. To enhance the authenticity of the urban traffic situation, real-time traffic videos are collected from the Bengaluru Traffic Management System. The video files were pre-processed by segmenting them, extracting frames from the video file, detecting objects, and then enriching content with meteorological data. The end product was a fully structured dataset that contained both frames and annotations. Data preparation placed great emphasis on the attempt to preserve (as much as possible) both the spatial and temporal characteristics of urban traffic activity. Ultimately, a rich and thorough dataset was developed, which allowed an accurate and contextual Ensemble Learning / AI model to be developed. The dataset was very important in allowing an accurate prediction and the examination of various features of traffic congestion behaviour across real-world urban environments.

3.2 Data Pre-processing and Feature Extraction

The steps for processing and generating features from traffic data are an important step in predictive modelling, especially for the task of traffic congestion prediction. Previous works have focused on structured traffic records or video-based data (i.e., Li et al., 2023; Cini & Aydin, 2024). However, most of these works did not employ both structured traffic data and video-based traffic scenes for a comprehensive traffic flow prediction model. The lack of research that investigates environmental data, visual data, and structured traffic data in the literature is a major limitation in the current understanding of traffic prediction flow. A joint investigation of environmental, visual, and structured traffic data could lead to more accurate predictions and could enhance theoretical understanding of congestion dynamics.

The purpose of this study was to investigate environmental and real-time visual traffic data, along with structured traffic records, to predict congestion. The data pre-processing and extraction process consisted of several different steps that cleaned, converted, and extracted relevant features from raw data. Each step was delineated to prepare the data for machine learning modelling. Figure 3 depicts the workflow for preparing traffic video data to enter the models. The workflow includes frame extraction using OpenCV, object detection for identifying vehicles and pedestrians, and feature extraction. The features in this step include object count, bounding box size, speed, and weather. The features become the input dataset for models to predict traffic congestion.

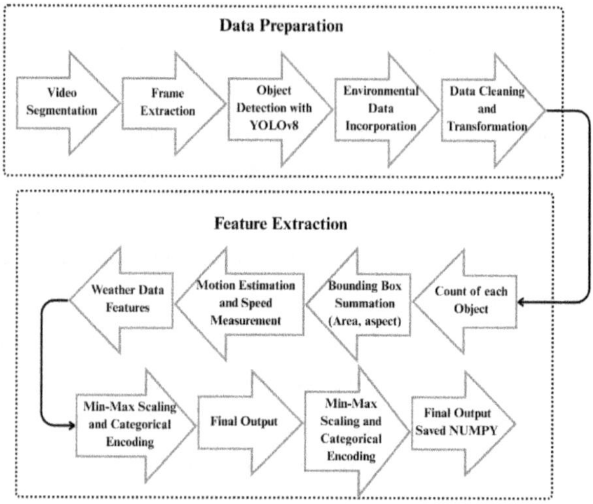

Figure 3: Data Pre-processing and Feature Extraction Workflow for Traffic Congestion Prediction

3.2.1 Data Preparation

The compilation of video-based data involved several necessary steps to transform raw video footage into usable datasets for future analysis. Video Segmentation, Frame Extraction, Object Detection with customised YOLOv8, Confidence Score Thresholding, Environmental Data Incorporation, and Data Cleaning and Transformation. The raw surveillance videos utilised in this study were incredibly large (~15 GB each) and were recorded in their raw, unedited form. The videos were captured over three days, from October 3 to October 5, and included both daytime and nighttime traffic conditions. The raw videos were manually segmented by the research team using VLC Media Player, and two different clip lengths were selected for comparative analysis: 2-minute segments and 5-second opening and closing segments. The segmented video clips were stored in the traffic_predictor/input_videos/ directory. Using OpenCV, extracted still frames were systematically collected from each segmented video at an extraction rate of one frame per second.

This provided a consistent temporal representation over the video segments without any interruptions or external movement. The finally extracted frames were stored in the output_data/frames/ directory. Frame-based processing has been previously used in traffic-based studies, but this process contributes to ensuring temporal consistency (Li et al., 2023).

Frames were taken from the video at regular intervals, and the customised YOLOv8 model was applied to undertake object detection on the video frames to detect traffic participants, which included cars, buses, trucks, two-wheelers, and pedestrians. The resulting object detections were stored in a .csv file (detection_results.csv) for further exploration and contained trackable variable information, including frame numbers, track number, object type, bounding box coordinates, and confidence score of each object detection in the video. Each of the video clips not only provided visual data for the study but also made it possible to obtain weather condition data (temperature, humidity level, and generalised weather) through the Open Weather Map API. This would permit not only the combination of video data and environmental or contextual conditions, but also the study of how environmental conditions impact traffic behavioural patterns. The dataset is therefore the combination of videos and weather information, which will be used to develop and evaluate the ensembles of deep learning models to predict traffic congestion.

Figure 4: Frame Extraction Overview for Traffic Video Data

Figure 4 provides the output of frame extraction via OpenCV. It shows one frame from the entire traffic image analysis video. This frame is used to do further processing tasks, like Object or vehicle detection and traffic analysis. Along with video-structured inputs, a structured CSV file was also created that included aggregated frame-specific statistics with the corresponding conditions of weather, as traffic_weather_data.csv. Each log contains entries with values that include counts of vehicles that were recorded, the average speed of those vehicles, temperature, humidity, and wind speed at the time of the records. Along with the first file, there was also a detection_results.csv file that logs the frame-by-frame outputs from customising the YOLOv8 Object Detection model, along with its frame number, type of object, confidence score, and bounding box. The CSV files will be essential moving forward through preprocessing and modelling, taking the form of temporal patterns and embedded contextual weather information for machine learning. The processed structured dataset was saved as a NumPy array format as files called (X_lstm.npy and y_lstm.npy) under the output_data/features/ directory to train and evaluate the Ensemble Learning model for predicting traffic congestion.

YOLOv8, a fast and accurate object detection model, was used to detect and classify many vehicles (such as cars, trucks, buses, motorcycles, and bicycles) and pedestrians from the extracted frames. YOLOv8's results were stored as a CSV file, labelled detection_results.csv, which contained the following fields for each detection: Frame number, detected object class, Bounding box (x, y; width, height), and Confidence score for the detection. To ensure that high-confidence detections were being used (prevention is better than the cure, as there will be much more information to work with than reject when finalising detection datasets), all detections with a confidence score below 0.5 were removed to minimise false positives. The confidence score threshold step is also a part of the object detection process, contributing to detection results accuracy verification, and determining reliable data for further analysis (Zhao et al., 2021).

Environmental data (such as weather) was collected and incorporated using the OpenWeatherMap API (OpenWeather, n.d.). Weather dimensions that corresponded to the video clips were extracted and added to the dataset. The attributes included: Temperature (°C), Humidity (%), and Weather condition (Clear, Cloudy, Rainy, Foggy). The weather data was merged with the object detection results, which provided a full dataset capable of predicting traffic jams. As part of data cleaning, outlier data points were parsed out of the data, such as very large bounding boxes (typically artefacts of incorrect detections). Duplicate records were merged, duplicate observations were dealt with, and missing records were filled to maintain dataset integrity. For the videos, instances of objects were counted per frame, and redundant detections in the frame were merged. These data cleaning methods are common to traffic prediction models for improving dataset quality. A portion of the extracted dataset with key object detection features and weather data is provided as an example in Appendix C.

3.2.2 Feature Extraction

Once the data had been prepared, features were extracted from both the visual data and associated contextual factors (the weather). The feature extraction process carried out several key steps to convert raw data into numerical, structured features that are used in machine learning models. The number of vehicles and pedestrians detected per frame was counted. This step produced several key features: Total number of vehicles per frame, Vehicle-to-pedestrian ratio, and Vehicle density over time. These features begin to account for traffic congestion and the interactions between vehicles and pedestrians, known to be important for determining accurate congestion predictions (Li et al., 2023). Bounding Box Summation: The width and height dimensions of each object's bounding box were utilised to derive the following additional features: Bounding box area and Aspect ratio (width/height) (Soom et al., 2024).

Coordinates of the centre of the bounding box. These features yield further insight into the size and location of objects, informing traffic flow and density. Motion Estimation and Speed Measurement: Since YOLOv8 was not guided towards object tracking, an additional logic was boiled down to estimate vehicle speed. A calculation between the x and y coordinates of the centroids of the bounding boxes from one frame compared to the next was then converted into a speed measurement. This is an important step to identify slow and fast-moving traffic, which is not a common feature in traffic prediction models. Weather Data features: Weather data was included as a feature directly for the traffic prediction model. The weather features were Temperature (a continuous variable), Humidity (a continuous variable), Weather condition (categorically encoded, e.g., Clear = 0, Cloudy = 1, Rain = 2). Weather features have been shown to impact traffic conditions and the predictive performance of traffic flow models or estimates of traffic behaviour.

Temporal and Spatial Features: Temporal features showed when traffic occurred, and were captured by categorising timestamps into bins that indicated what time of day (e.g., Morning, Afternoon, Evening, Night) the timestamp represented, to understand the variation in traffic and what might explain it sometimes. Spatial features can be thought of as surveillance locations serving as examples in fixed locations to show how congestion appeared spatially.

Feature Scaling and Encoding: Continuous features (e.g., bounding box areas, object counts, and speed estimates) were all Min-Max scaled to keep them on a similar scale before putting them in any machine learning model. The categorical features used (e.g, weather condition) were one-hot encoded. The final dataset is contained in the following NumPy arrays: X_lstm.npy - Feature matrix containing all the numerical and encoded attributes, y_lstm.npy - Target labels representing congestion categories or counts. These arrays were saved in the output_data/features/ folder and were to be the final structured dataset for deep learning-based models for traffic prediction research. The Python script that was employed for deep feature extraction, using the chosen convolutional neural network model, is presented in Appendix D.

3.2.2.1 Constructing the Traffic Flow Matrix

By repeatedly running each deep learning model (base learner) at various periods, the ideal time delays are determined, meaning that the number of steps in the previous traffic flow determines the current traffic flow. As a result, the ideal time lag is determined for every base learner, set L hours as the time lag, and add L additional features, each of which shows hourly traffic volumes in an L-h period. Using data from the past L hours, prediction models attempt to forecast the traffic volume in the $L + 1^{th}$Ur. (Ponce et al., 2020), The model used for a range of horizon values is examined. For single-step prediction, the prediction horizon h is 1, while for multistep prediction, it is 6,12,24 forecasts (short-term forecast, that is). In other words, the next hour(s) traffic flow value using prior W-hour data (Cini and Aydin, 2024) is predicted. Consequently, the traffic flow matrix as input (*X*) and output (*Y*) matrix is built as follows:

$$X = \begin{bmatrix} f_t & f_{t+1} & \cdots & f_{t+L-1} \\ f_{t+1} & f_{t+2} & \cdots & f_{t+L} \\ \vdots & \vdots & \ddots & \vdots \\ f_{t+d} & f_{t+d+1} & \cdots & f_{t+L-1+d} \end{bmatrix} \quad (4)$$

$$Y_h = \begin{bmatrix} f_{t+L} & f_{t+L+1} & \cdots & f_{t+L+h-1} \\ f_{t+L+1} & f_{t+L+2} & \cdots & f_{t+L+h} \\ \vdots & \vdots & \ddots & \vdots \\ f_{t+L+d} & f_{t+L+d+1} & \cdots & f_{t+L+d+h-1} \end{bmatrix} \quad (5)$$

In Equations 4 and 5, f_t: traffic volume at the time t. L : The number of past hours used as lag features, h: number of future hours to predict (prediction horizon), d: number of training samples (sliding windows) and each row in Y_h: Represents the future time steps corresponding to the input row in X.

3.3 Model Development

The traffic congestion prediction model uses an Ensemble Deep Learning Approach (EDLA) that describes the stacked models, such as MLP, SVC, and CNN-LSTM, and uses the meta-learner to extract the best predictions and improve an ensemble learning approach. Comparison Models give the reader a basis for comparison for the ensemble methods and standard models, such as Random Forest, KNN, and SVR. The training and evaluation processes for both approaches are also discussed. Afterwards, the hyperparameter tuning and optimisation methods are discussed after the model was constrained within the ensemble approaches. The last part of the report is about the incorporation of weather data and some of the feature engineering steps that were included to effectively improve the predictive accuracy of the models in this report.

3.3.1 Ensemble Deep Learning Approach

Ensemble deep learning is an advanced form of machine learning modelling involving multiple learners (models) that complement each other to improve predictive performance, robustness, and generalizability (Rane et al., 2024). Unlike single models, which represent a particular viewpoint, ensemble methods aggregate the predictions of several models, making them far superior methods to use in practice that are far less prone to overfitting and underfitting, and offer more reliable outputs. In deep learning, ensembles usually involve combining different neural networks or classifiers that capture distinct features from the patterns inherent in complex data (Veres & Moussa, 2019). Ensemble deep learning has become especially valuable for predicting road congestion and traffic flow, particularly because traffic data is multifaceted, dynamic, and affected by a variety of variables, including environmental alternatives, vehicle densities, road infrastructure, and driver behaviour. Models alone generally do not capture all of the variability in heterogeneous data; therefore, an ensemble method reduces error by leveraging the complex relationships learnt from the data with all of the models' attributes combined, thus additionally improving prediction stability and robustness.

Various ensemble learning methods have been applied to traffic congestion prediction with success. For example, Wang et al. 2025 used convolutional neural networks (CNNs) to identify traffic congestion across a range of real-world scenarios and reported the benefits of using deep models to extract spatial features. While developing a novel ensemble learning mechanism to forecast urban traffic congestion, researchers found significant improvements in forecasting accuracy shown through model aggregation vs. a single-model baseline. (Shabbir et al. 2024) also able to develop a stacking-based ensemble deep learning traffic management system based on acoustic-based detection of vehicles in smart cities, which showed the efficacy of ensemble methods in real-time use cases in smart cities. Finally, investigated machine learning and big data approaches for predicting real-time traffic congestion and reinforced the need for ensemble measures to deal with massive and high-dimensional traffic datasets.

3.3.1.1 Data Flow Structure of the Ensemble Deep Learning Model

The architecture of the model for traffic congestion prediction is depicted in Figure 5. The data flow diagram of the model outlines the architecture that receives raw traffic video data and returns estimates on the level of traffic congestion for specific time intervals. This workflow consists of a structured sequence of processing stages and shows the sequence through which raw traffic video data goes through transformations and refinements before it is sent to the ensemble learning model.

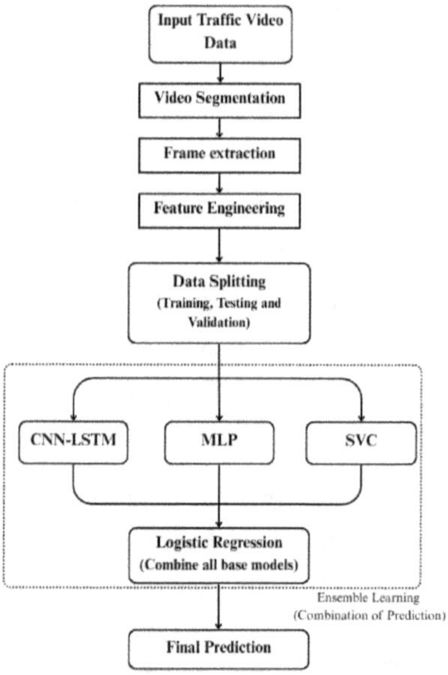

Figure 5: Data Flow Structure of the Ensemble Deep Learning Model

a) Input Traffic Video Data

The workflow begins with the collection of raw traffic surveillance video as the input. The raw videos usually come from fixed-mounted cameras placed on road intersections or highways. These videos input visual data on traffic as it moves or builds up in density.

b) Video Segmentation

The unbroken video stream is segmented into smaller time-defined clips to allow manageable analysis. Video segmentation allows consistent processing in the next stages of the workflow and is used for parallel processing where applicable, such that each segment represents a time window that will help track the levels of traffic congestion in the video. Video segmentation was done manually using the convert/save function in VLC Media Player to extract clips that were time-defined.

c) Frames Extraction

When an input video is filmed, the resulting video clip must be subjected to a new stage consisting of frames being extracted from the video clip at fixed time intervals (each 1 second, for example). The resulting frames represent static paintings of the traffic interaction and movements, which are used to identify and extract the moving or stationary objects (vehicles, cyclists, pedestrians, etc.) in the scene to begin an analysis. Frame extraction was performed with the help of OpenCV, which allowed frame selection that was accurate and time-specific.

d) Feature Engineering

Once the frames are extracted, an object detection process is applied. The resulting images are repurposed for the feature engineering stage, which results in features that are processed in further analysis. Features such as the count and the types of objects (cars, buses, and trucks of various sizes), bounding box size, average speed estimates, weather (temperature, humidity), and geographical-based traffic densities are analysed in more detail. The engineered features to be used as inputs to the predictive models represent an amalgamation of the visual infrastructure and environments, and the influence of congestion on all roads. Feature engineering made use of the YOLOv8 model for object detection and Python (Pandas, NumPy) to organise and transform the extracted features.

e) Data Splitting

After all of the stages of deriving the feature set dataset, the dataset is split into three samplings: train, validate, and test. The splitting of data ensures that information is taken from one sampling of the data to train, then a part of the dataset is used to validate the model parameters, and finally, the use of the testing data would give a generalisation performance of the expected traffic congestion predictions. Stratified sampling is used to maintain balanced distributions in classes.

f) Base Learners

CNN-LSTM, MLP, and SVC. Three different models will be used as base learners, simultaneously and as parallel predictors, so that the different learning characteristics are combined.

The CNN-LSTM model combines Convolutional Neural Networks (CNN) for the retrieval of spatial features from the images, and Long Short-Term Memory (LSTM) for capturing time dependencies across sequences of visual representations. This learner is helpful, especially for processing video frame sequences of visual data (video).

A Multilayer Perceptron (MLP) is employed as a dense, fully connected neural network to learn complex nonlinear mappings in the structured, feature combination data.

Support Vector Classifier (SVC) is attractive for its performance in high-dimensional spaces, as it is used to avoid overfitting smaller datasets. Each model operates on the same input features independently to produce first-round predictions regarding the level of traffic congestion.

g) Meta Learner (Logistic Regression)

The outputs from the base learners (CNN-LSTM, MLP, and SVC) created above are forwarded to the meta learning model based on Logistic Regression. This meta-learning model integrates these initial or base predictions via ensemble stacking methods. The Logistic Regression meta-learner puts the appropriate weights on each prediction from each base learner and outputs a final consolidated prediction. Ensemble predictions have a reduction of bias from the individual model predictions, and their performance may improve.

h) Final Prediction

The final output of the Logistic Regression meta-learner is the final prediction and the representation of the system. This output is in terms of High, Medium, or Low congestion, based on the individual probabilities on which the ensemble predicted, as well as the decision thresholds. The model represented the current level of traffic congestion alongside the causal traffic patterns and future traffic conditions. This enabled more nuanced decisions and was used to make traffic management systems.

3.3.1.2 Architecture of Ensemble Deep Learning Model

This study uses the stacking-based method in which outputs from different base learners are combined to achieve improved final performance. It utilises a meta-learner that will generate outputs resulting from multiple models and ultimately learns how to weight the individual contributions of its models. Specifically, the developed model utilises outputs from a multi-layer perceptron classifier (MLP), a support-vector classifier (SVC), and a hybrid CNN-LSTM, and inputs these into a logistic regression learner (meta-learner). As an ensemble stack, the developed model can take advantage of the MLP, SVC, and CNN-LSTM's ability to capture complex spatial-temporal differentiable and feature-based relationships in traffic data to more accurately predict congestion.

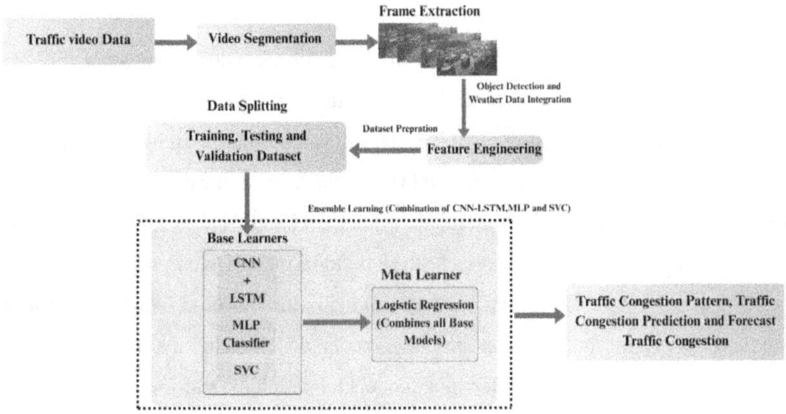

Figure 6: Architecture of the Ensemble Model for Traffic Congestion Prediction

Figure 6 shows the Architecture of the model, which identifies the steps of how traffic video data is pre-processed through frame extraction and object detection. The remaining features, including object count, speed, and weather information, were plugged directly into base models (MLP, SVC, CNN-LSTM). The base models are combined using an ensemble, combined with a meta-learner for traffic congestion classification (Low, Medium, High).

In this research, an ensemble deep learning method predicts traffic congestion with a combination of base learners, including a Multi-Layer Perceptron Classifier (MLP), a Support Vector Classifier (SVC), and a CNN-LSTM model. These models processed the extracted features independently, based on the traffic video data and other external weather data, to yield outputs that were input into the meta-learner (Logistic Regression) for producing predictions. The ensemble process can be expressed mathematically as follows: In Equation 6, the ensemble learning prediction. Open $\hat{y}$ presented as

$$\hat{y} = F(h_1(x), h_2(x), \dots \dots h_n(x)) \tag{6}$$

Where: x is the input feature vector, $h_1, h_2, \dots . h_n$ Present the individual base models, F is the combination function (e.g., a meta-learner like logistic regression) that integrates the predictions of all base models to produce the final prediction $\hat{y}$.

Here, the combination function F learns how to effectively combine the individual outputs to minimise the overall prediction error. Thus, the Ensemble approach provides a powerful solution by combining diverse models' strengths, making it highly suitable for handling the complexity and dynamic nature of real-world traffic congestion prediction.

The proposed model is viewed as an ensemble deep learning model since it is a hybrid model that incorporates both machine learning and deep learning models under a model architecture. The machine learning base classifiers included in the ensemble are Support Vector Classifier (SVC) and Multilayer Perceptron (MLP), which act as the classifiers, while the deep learning model, CNN-LSTM, learn complex spatial-temporal patterns as presented in video-based traffic data. The model pseudo-stacks the individual models as output predictions through logistic regression into a meta-learner model, allowing the model to take into consideration each base model's contributions. The ensemble model, which includes a deep-learning model to process video data and machine-learning models for structured traffic and weather features, captures a holistic interpretation of traffic behaviour. Therefore, it meets the ensemble deep learning model definition.

3.3.1.3 Base Models and Meta Learner

The performance of ensemble learning largely depends on the effectiveness of its base models and the meta-learner that combines their predictions. In this study, three distinct base models are employed to capture different aspects of the traffic data: the Multi-Layer Perceptron (MLP) classifier, the Support Vector Classifier (SVC), and the CNN-LSTM hybrid model. These models are selected due to their complementary strengths in handling different types of traffic data, each offering a unique contribution to the overall prediction process.

The base model is a single learning algorithm for making predictions by using some features (or a representation of data). These predictions are then aggregated to form a final prediction in an ensemble model. The purpose of this study is to use the MLP classifier, SVC, and CNN-LSTM as baseline classifiers.

The MLP is a feedforward neural network created to model nonlinear relationships among input features. MLP could become useful for modelling complex interactions for structured knowledge using traffic data, as defined by the many features, time of day, weather, and traffic density through time.

The SVC is a powerful supervised learning algorithm that performs well in higher-dimensional spaces. In addition to being able to determine the optimal hyperplanes, an SVC would be able to help distinguish the levels of congestion in traffic flow, given noise, and how well datasets are balanced.

The CNN-LSTM model is designed to capture the multiple spatial and temporal dependencies of traffic data in videos. The CNN will extract spatial features from video traffic frames, and the LSTM will model the temporal evolution of each spatial feature, which allows the model to capture the dynamic nature of changes in traffic behaviour across time.

Meta-Learner (Logistic Regression) uses base models' results or predictions as a way to improve prediction performance as an ensemble learning technique. In this ensemble, the meta-learner is a Logistic Regression model, which takes the outputs from the base model as its inputs and combines these to make the final prediction. Logistic Regression is used as the meta-learner because it is simple, interpretable, and efficient with the amount of data it requires to learn a linear decision boundary from the base models' predictions. Logistic regression is particularly useful in cases where the aim is to aggregate the output of base models in a way that weighs their contributions to the best outcome, which is most useful when the base models have opposing strengths and weaknesses. Having trained base models along with a meta-learner enables a complete and comprehensive method to predict traffic congestion, because each model provides their contribution to the whole decision-making process.

3.3.1.4 Function of Base Learners in the Ensemble Model

Base learners are the fundamental components of an ensemble learning model because base learners learn their distinct patterns in the input data and produce intermediate predictions.

Each base learner is trained in parallel over the same dataset, but each is trained with differing learning assumptions, ideal for each specific type of feature or representation of the data. The different base learners help position lone learner models at a disadvantage in capturing the complexities of relationships in the data compared to the ensemble model. These intermediate predictions made by the base learners are brought together by the meta-learner to make a final prediction. In this study, three base learners are utilised: Multilayer Perceptron (MLP Classifier), Support Vector Classifier (SVC), and CNN-LSTM. The following sections will present each model's architecture, operational mechanics, and individual roles in the ensemble model.

Convolutional Neural Network with LSTM (CNN-LSTM)

The CNN-LSTM model is a composite deep learning model that combines Convolutional Neural Networks (CNN) for spatial feature extraction and Long Short-Term Memory (LSTM) networks for time-based sequence learning. The model can process. Time series data extracted from frames of traffic videos. Input features. Sequences of frames from traffic videos sampled at regular time intervals, detected objects with their corresponding attributes per frame (i.e., size of the bounding box, class of object), and Temporal patterns of data regarding the movement of vehicles across the frames.

The CNN component of the model will perform spatial feature extraction on each of the single frames. However, in a video, each frame is just one instance of a traffic scene, and CNNs will extract the prominent objects within the traffic scenes, for example, cars, traffic lanes, and pedestrians, etc. The CNN layers will carry out convolutions, where convolutional filters will derive spatial patterns. These filters are learned filters and will allow the model to extract potentially complex patterns like vehicle density, roadway conditions, and other traffic-dependent parameters. The CNN module uses a sequence of convolutional operations followed by pooling operations that will reduce the dimension of the input frames while capturing the more pertinent features of the input frames.

Upon the CNN extracting spatial features for the frame sequence, the spatial features are then delivered to the LSTM layers to capture the temporal dynamics. The LSTM is great for sequential data and can learn from video frames over time, where the ordering of the video frames and the temporal transition between the frames are important. The LSTM networks are capable of learning the relationship between consecutive frames, allowing the model to learn how congestion has changed through time. For example, the model might learn that the area of congestion in the following few frames is concerning the vehicles present in the previous few frames or the road conditions in the prior video frames.

Predicting the Congestion Levels When the CNN has learnt the spatial feature, and the LSTMs have learnt the temporal dependencies, the output layer of the complete network can predict the congestion level based on the learnt spatial-temporal features. This could either be a classification, for example, low, medium, or high traffic congestion, based on the severity of the traffic congestion. Occasionally, this could also be a regression prediction, predicting a continuous value for congestion, which will depend on how the model has been set up. Most designs either use a softmax activation function in the output layer for a prediction based on multiple classes or a sigmoid activation function for a prediction based on two classes. Extract spatial features for each frame, capturing whether an object is present in the frame, where it is in the layout of the frame, and the density of vehicles in the frame. Capture the sequence of CNN feature maps over time and learn temporal dependencies and trends with traffic flow. This combination allows the model to detect patterns related to congestion that evolve based on movement and vehicle dynamics. How it acts on the ensemble: The CNN-LSTM extracts a rich spatio-temporal representation from the video data, one that cannot be learned with a structured model like MLP and SVC. The CNN-LSTM adds a deep learning aspect of visual raw data to the model and improves how the model learns to predict congestion in real time.

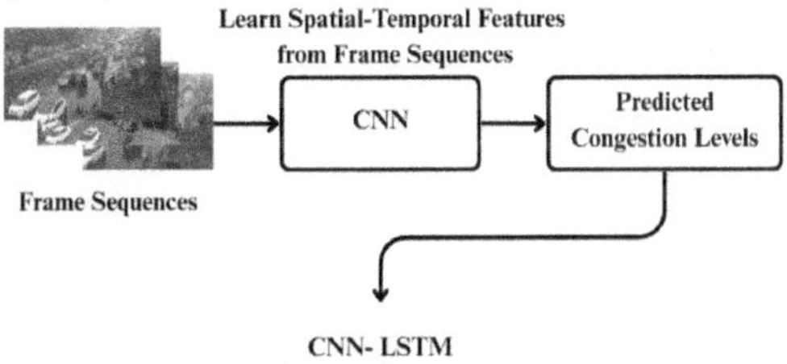

Figure 7: CNN-LSTM Architecture for Spatial-Temporal Feature Learning and Congestion Prediction

Figure 7 shows the CNN-LSTM architecture designed to extract spatial and temporal features of traffic from video data (Designed by the researcher as part of this study). Spatial features are extracted from the video frames with the Convolutional Neural Network (CNN), and temporal dependencies are captured by the Long Short-Term Memory (LSTM) network; both methods combined allow for an effective prediction of traffic congestion to be based on an understanding of the spatial layout of where the data originates, and the time series movement in time.

Multilayer Perceptron (MLP Classifier)

The Multilayer Perceptron (MLP Classifier) is a supervised learning algorithm that consists of a directed graph with multiple layers of interconnected nodes. It is a feed-forward artificial neural network and is well-suited for structured/tabular data. The first layer of an MLP is the input layer, where the data is passed into the network. Here, each feature (e.g., traffic volume, weather conditions, and time of day) corresponds to an input neuron. Thus, the number of neurons in the input layer corresponds to the number of features in the traffic dataset. For example, if the dataset contains traffic volume, weather, and time, each feature corresponds to an input neuron. Overall engineered numeric features: Vehicle counts per frame, Average speed, Weather features, such as temperature and humidity, Object density attributes from video frames.

MLP often has one or more hidden layers where the critical learning and pattern recognition happen. Hidden layers are fully connected to the prior layer and the subsequent layer. The number of neurons in the hidden layers is not fixed, and typically, deeper networks, which include more hidden layers, can learn and recognise more complex patterns. In a linear transformation, each neuron in a hidden layer is doing a weighted summation of the inputs it received from the prior layer. The weights are the parameters that the network learns as it gets trained. After the linear transformation, an activation function is applied to introduce non-linearity. Common activation functions are ReLU (Rectified Linear Unit) and Sigmoid. For several reasons, ReLU is often used since it avoids the vanishing gradient problem and speeds up convergence.

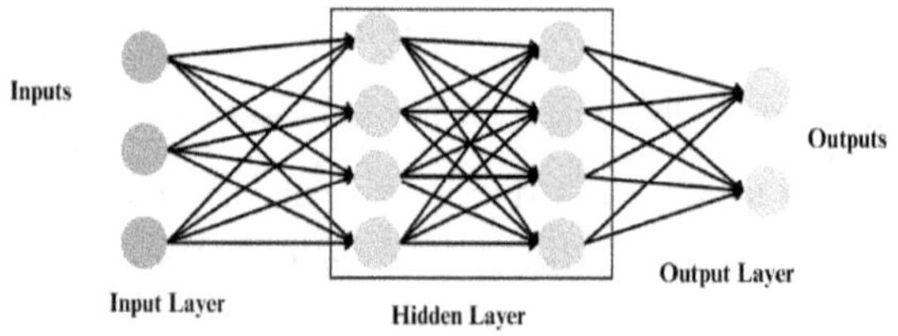

Figure 8: Multi-Layer Perceptron

The structure of the Multi-Layer Perceptron (MLP), which is one of the base learners in the traffic congestion prediction model, is shown in Figure 8 (Adapted from Awan, A. A., et al., 2024). An MLP has an input layer, any number of hidden layers, and an output layer. The MLP is trained to learn and find non-linear relationships from the learnt and engineered features to create predictions based on non-linear relationships.

The ending of the network is the output layer, comprised of one or more neurons that generate the predictions. For traffic congestion prediction, the output layer alternatively could have a single neuron predicting congested vs not congested (binary classification) or several neurons as part of a multi-class prediction describing the state of congestion (i.e., low, medium, high). The activation functions in the output layer are softmax for multi-class or sigmoid for binary; these functions give the network a probabilistic prediction of the outputs by normalising the output of the layer to a sum of one for the predicted probabilities.

The MLP Classifier has an input layer that takes the feature vector, one or more hidden layers that use non-linear functions (e.g., RELU), and an output layer that produces probabilities of the resultant classes of congestion (Low, Medium, High). The MLP Classifier during training is minimising cross-entropy loss through backpropagation and stochastic gradient descent (or Adam optimiser), and the weights were updated accordingly. The MLP Classifier model models more complex non-linear relationships between features and output classes. Therefore, the MLP Classifier is a good fit for classifying traffic congestion based on engineered statistical features.

The multi-layer perceptron, or MLP, is a feedforward neural network with many learning layers that can detect complex and non-linear relationships in the data. The MLP will be most effective in the context of structured traffic data when there are several features, such as traffic volumes, weather, time of day, and historical data, that work in multi-dimensional ways. Data will enter through the input layer and move into multiple hidden layers through forward propagation. At each neuron, the weighted sum of inputs will be calculated and the activation function applied to the weighted sum. This process is repeated until the output layer is reached and the MLP provides a prediction of a level of traffic congestion.

Once the data has passed through the MLP and produced outputs, the MLP will compute a similar loss function (e.g., cross-entropy loss for when classes are being predicted) to define the degree of error in the forecasts of traffic congestion, where the error is defined as the difference between the forecast traffic congestion levels (as predicted by the MLP) with the actual/true/observed level of traffic congestion. After this forward pass, and before the back-propagation is done to update the MLP weights, the MLP will calculate a gradient of the loss function with respect to each weight in the MLP. The weights are then updated using an optimisation algorithm (e.g., Gradient Descent and Adam) to minimise loss. The forward-backwards process continues through multiple epochs and until convergence. The MLP can learn complex patterns and tricky dependencies between the features. Model outputs are then provided to the meta-learner to weight the level of statistical trends of travel behaviour in transportation.

Support Vector Classifier (SVC)

The Support Vector Classifier (SVC) is a supervised learning, margin-based algorithm that addresses normative classification tasks. SVC can function in high dimensions, and either uses a superhuman ability to identify class boundaries using linear separation (for linear classification), or uses the help of kernel functions for non-linear classification, if the class features are separable. The LSTM network can process frames of video temporally, and through this process, can understand the temporal dynamics of traffic flow (i.e., as a video). The output of the LSTM is one or more feature vectors that represent those learned patterns that are based on the temporal dependencies. The feature vectors from the LSTM have been flattened for structural compatibility with the SVC, and that is the input to the SVC model. The flattened LSTM features were merged into a single fixed-size input vector containing four features for each instance of traffic data. Input Features, SVC works on the same tabular input features as the MLP Classifier, Counts of Objects, Speed characteristics, Bounding box characteristics, and Weather characteristics. The SVC model finds an optimal hyperplane (decision boundary) to optimally separate the different classes of traffic congestion (e.g., Low, Medium, High).

SVC is primarily based on the core concept of maximising the margin between classes at support vectors, the only points from the classes that matter. Starting from the support vectors allows SVC to generalise to unseen data and prevent the danger of overfitting. In cases where the data is not linearly separable in its feature space, SVC can use the kernel trick to project the input features into a higher-dimensional space where a linear boundary can be found. The common kernels are: linear, polynomial, and RBF (Radial Basis Function) kernels, and allow for non-linear separations using a complex traffic data set. The features produced from the flattened LSTM layer are being fed to the SVC, which preserves sequential dependencies in traffic flow information (i.e., the past traffic condition and the latter congestion). SVC can take features to define a decision boundary that classifies traffic into various congestion levels. SVC uses the training data to optimise the hyperplane to classify traffic data into different classes.

The decision boundaries defined by SVC are dependent on the LSTM features, which contain temporal patterns in traffic information. This allows SVC to classify traffic as congested, using information about the current and past traffic flow.

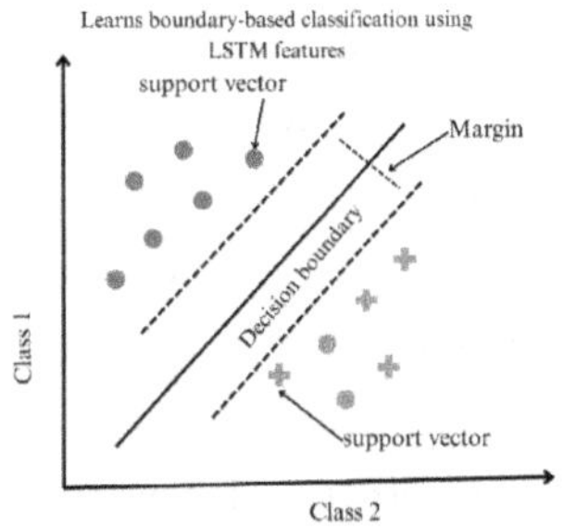

Figure 9: SVC (Support Vector Classifier)

Figure 9 shows the Support Vector Classifier (SVC) in the model and serves as one of the base learners for traffic congestion prediction (Researcher's illustration). The SVC is trained on the extracted features from the traffic video data, after which it classifies the congestion level (Low, Medium, High) based on the patterns and relationships associated with the features in the matrix.

SVC ideally calculates a hyperplane where the margin of separation is maximised to designate different classes of congestion. If the data isn't linearly separable, it uses a kernel trick (for example, Radial Basis Function kernel), which projects the data into a higher-dimensional space where separating the classes is possible. The model is then trained to classify the traffic state into one of the defined classes based on a geometrical position within feature space. SVC will provide a strong classification by maximising the margin of separation between the various congestion classes, which makes it robust and less sensitive to outliers. The distinct contributions of each base learner provide unique perspectives into the data set through MLP as a source of non-linear tabular feature scenery, SVC, an instance of example-based scenario mapping, and CNN-LSTM using video and dynamic sequence modelling. Overall, the set of output parameters produced by each of these base learners forms a diverse set of features and information for the meta-learner. Meta-learners have several advantages, e.g., improved ensemble accuracy and robustness in predicting levels of traffic congestion under various intersection conditions.

3.3.1.5 Function of Meta-Learner (Logistic Regression) in the Ensemble Model

In this ensemble deep learning architecture, a meta-learning layer is used to configure the predictions output from the ensemble of base learners. In the case of this research, Logistic Regression was used as a meta-learner due to logistic regression being easy to interpret, simple in terms of the mathematics involved, and effective in synthesising the output of multiple models in a classification context. The meta-learner is trained not on the original features of the dataset, but rather on the outputs generated by the base models in this architecture, specifically the MLP Classifier, SVC, and CNN-LSTM. Each base learner was first developed on the training dataset using k-fold (usually 5-fold or higher) cross-validation to train each of the models. While training the base learners with k-fold cross-validation, the out-of-fold predictions were collected in each iteration. The out-of-fold predictions are used to generate a new feature space, or what is referenced in this study as the "meta-feature matrix"; subsequently, this new meta-feature matrix will be given as the input to the meta-learner.

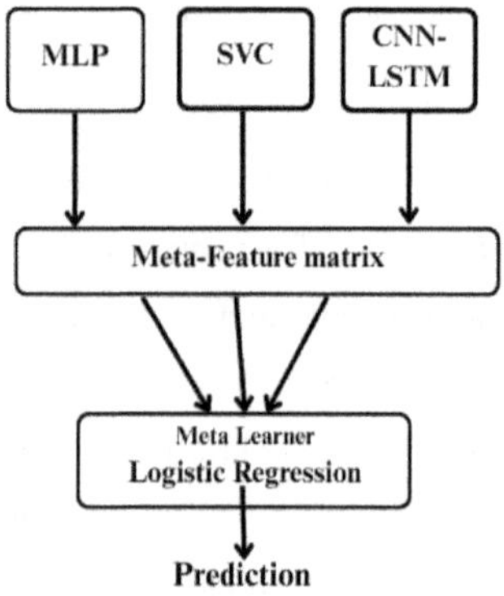

Figure 10: Ensemble Framework Using Logistic Regression as Meta-Learner

In Figure 10, the ensemble framework is shown, which combines multiple base models (i.e., MLP, SVC, and CNN-LSTM) to create the final ensemble (Researcher's illustration). The outputs of the base models will be input into the Logistic Regression meta-learner, which will combine the outputs and then provide a final traffic congestion prediction, thereby improving the accuracy and robustness of the model overall.

Three base classifiers are used, and each training instance in the meta-feature space is represented by three values, whereby each value corresponds to the class probability (or predicted outputs) of one of the base models. The meta-learner finds the optimal combination of these predictions to ultimately make a classification. The meta-learner is ultimately learning how much to trust each of the base models in particular situations based on their prior performance patterns.

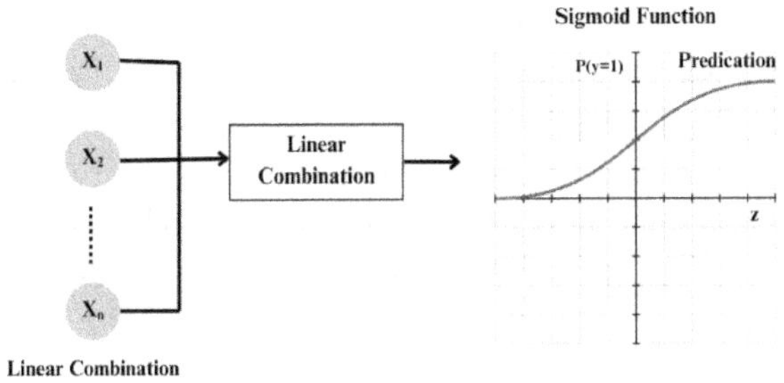

Figure 11: Logistic Regression Showing Feature Combination and Sigmoid Activation

Figure 11 shows the conceptual design for the use of Logistic Regression (Researcher's illustration). Where the features from the base models are combined and stored as a single long vector to put into a linear equation. All of this information was passed through the Sigmoid activation function, where it was received as a probability value estimating traffic congestion classification (Low, Medium, or High).

Logistic Regression, as a linear model, assigns weights to the base model predictions to learn the best combination of these. During the testing phase, all base model class predictions for unseen instances are provided to the trained Logistic Regression model, which outputs a class prediction, typically a discrete class label in this case (Low, Medium, or High congestion level). The two-level learning approach improves the generalisation of the ensemble as well as capitalises on the complementary strengths of the base models.

CNN part of CNN-LSTM captures the spatial structure and dependency of the road network. CNN learns traffic images like localised slowdown/queue patterns that spread through adjacent road segments. LSTM part of CNN-LSTM captures temporal dynamics (rush-hour) cycles, incident effects. It keeps short-term and long-term memory, capturing periodicity and sudden trend shifts. MLP processes tabular/contextual variables (weather, calendar events, incident flags). It processes heterogeneous, non-sequential features. SVC captures rare, highly non-linear situations (accident on a feeder road, holiday exodus). It carves sharp decision boundaries on small, tricky subsets. Overall forecast is performed by the logistic regression meta-learner that learns optimal weights for the outputs. This fulfils the first objective of the research.

CNN-LSTM performed a great job at capturing spatio-temporal features (e.g., location + time series of traffic). MLP (Multi-Layer Perceptron) was effective in learning non-linear patterns from numerical and categorical traffic data. SVM did an effective job on small to medium dataset ranges with classification-level-based congestion.

So, the second objective of the thesis achieves the results via a stacking ensemble architecture with CNN-LSTM, MLP, and SVM as base learners and Logistic Regression as a meta-learner.

CNN layer pinpoints critical road segments or junction hot spots. LSTM captures temporal attention. It reveals lead-leg effects (like rainfall 15 min earlier spikes congestion. MLP gives ranks to weather variables, event flags, school holiday dummies, etc. SVC captures surface edge-case scenarios like low-volume and high-delay incidents. Logistic regression meta-learner shows which learner dominates under specific contexts. Together, these techniques satisfy the requirement to identify relevant objects like roads, incidents, weather states, and recognise patterns that signal forthcoming congestion. This achieves the third objective of the research.

3.3.2 Experiment Setup

Throughout the evaluation of the ensemble deep learning model, this research needed baseline models to compare against. The baseline models will come from a variety of traditional machine learning models, as well as deep learning models, with the ensemble deep learning model, such as CNN-LSTM, MLP (Multi-Layer Perceptron) Classifier, SVC (Support Vector Classifier), and the Logistic Regression meta learner. For deep learning models, the models were implemented using TensorFlow 2 and Keras; however, for the machine learning models, and built using scikit-learn, which has a complete set of helpers for model training, evaluation, and cross-validation. When each model is configured to best allow for fair and reasonable comparisons.

The CNN-LSTM model had to include a 1D convolutional layer, which contained 64 filters and a kernel size of 3, ReLU for the activation, and a dropout layer of 0.2 to address overfitting. Furthermore, the LSTM layer configured had 128 units and was connected to a Dense (fully-connected) layer, containing 64 units, which was then connected to the output layer using softmax (as an activation). Model training made use of the Adam optimiser, with a batch size of 8, epochs of 15, and a 20% validation split (plus early stopping). Early stopping helps prevent excessive training and overfitting by halting the process once performance on the validation data stops improving.

The MLP Classifier had 2 hidden layers, containing 128 and 64 neurons with the ReLU activation function. The Adam solver was used on the model, with a maximum number of 500 iterations, and a random state of 42 to enhance replicability.

The SVC model was fitted with an RBF kernel and then enabled probability estimates since it was a key feature for the ensemble-based meta-level classification.

Lastly, the meta-learner used was Logistic Regression, with a multinomial strategy, LBFGS solver, and a maximum number of iterations set to 1000. In this case, ensured that every model had a fair chance to perform and optimise, and allowed for a reasonable comparison against the ensemble method in this research.

3.3.2.1 Hardware and Software Requirements and Configuration

All models and scripts were executed on a personal computing system with an Intel® Core™ i5-1135G7 processor (4 cores, 8 threads), at 2.40 GHz, with 8 GB of DDR4 RAM, and 512 GB of SSD storage. The system had Intel Iris® Xe Graphics (integrated) and ran Windows 11 Home (64-bit). This configuration was sufficient for performing the activities involved with the short-term traffic prediction tasks, object detection applied to short video clips, and training light-to-moderate-sized deep learning models. When training and executing models, efficient memory allocation and smaller batch sizes were employed to leverage the effectiveness of the personal computing system (Hassanien et al. 2024).

a) Programming Language and IDEs

Python 3.9, the entire research pipeline was implemented using Python 3.9 - a suitable programming language because of its diverse and comprehensive ecosystem of libraries for video processing, data management and manipulation, and machine learning. Python's simplicity and ease of readability aided development speed, particularly in terms of developing the multiple components of the pipeline concurrently. Additionally, Python's open-source nature and extensive community support gave the implementation a good basis to build upon. Visual Studio Code (VS Code) was the main integrated development environment used to write and maintain Python scripts. VS Code was helpful because of its lightweight nature, extension marketplace, and integration with Git for easy management of code and debugging. VS Code also offered easy navigation between modules and organised development in separate areas of the project.

Jupyter Notebook from the Anaconda distribution was used as the interactive development environment for development and experimentation. Jupyter Notebook was particularly useful for exploratory data analysis, training machine learning models, and visualising the intermediate and final results. The modularity of notebooks enabled the documentation of the common steps of each experiment and could be reused, which assists reproducibility and facilitates iterations for tuning and improvement of the final model.

b) Data Processing and Machine Learning Libraries

NumPy was one of the core libraries used in this research to facilitate high-performance numerical calculations and computations. It has capabilities for multi-dimensional arrays and lots of functions to work with the data, which requires the ability to manipulate and analyse large-scale datasets historically and in real-time. NumPy was used to represent the time series sequences of traffic-related variables and fast matrices. The ability of NumPy to facilitate rapid matrix operations is what is required for a data matrix. The input in traffic flow models was used to build the model, and it was an essential part of many of the feature engineering. In this study, NumPy was able to make calculating different outputs in computationally heavy machinery much faster.

Pandas was used as the primary tool of choice for manipulating and preprocessing data because it showed its flexibility when handling structured data. It was especially valuable in dealing with the output generated from the object detection post-processing at the frame level, so it was easy to handle the detection outputs and join other data sources (e.g., weather, etc.) with detection results by aligning on time and other key IDs required for sorting. Pandas is a powerful package that can create a Data-Frame to allow for filtering, grouping, joining, and reshaping your data to produce clean, structured datasets that are suitable for training and evaluating models using machine learning algorithms. Furthermore, scikit-learn's coupling with visualisation and analysis libraries for general dataset exploration assisted with the visualisation and exploration of characteristics of the datasets.

Scikit-learn is an extensive machine learning library and is written in Python, and is utilised a lot for building traditional regression-based baseline models. The regressors were typically Linear Regression (LR), Decision Tree Regressor (DT), Random Forest Regressor (RF), Support Vector Regressor (SVR), and K-Nearest Neighbours Regressor (KNN) models, which were developed and evaluated using scikit-learn. The library allowed using built-in functions for splitting data, cross-validation application, scaling features, and obtaining some metric evaluations for performance, such as mean squared error and R^2 score. In addition, it was utilised to build out the meta-learner in the ensemble model using logistic regression, and its modular nature and the alignment with NumPy and Pandas vastly aided the development of conventional models and comparison to the ensemble deep learning approach proposed.

c) Deep Learning Frameworks

TensorFlow and Keras are the deep learning frameworks used for designing, building, and training neural network models. TensorFlow is an honoured Google project that can take any large machine learning process, including training and inference, and keep it flexible and efficient. The ability to deploy models to numerous environments, including local machines, clouds, and cloud infrastructures, means there is space for considerable scalability and performance as models are being created, developed, and evaluated. While neural network models can be created using pure TensorFlow.

Keras is a high-level neural network API that utilises TensorFlow as the backbone for low-level operations. A majority of the deep learning and experimentation could not be done without Keras, as Keras simplified and helped bring clarity to development and experimentation. Keras incorporates a very intuitive and informal syntax with a modular method, making it possible to quickly think and build complex models and accomplish this in a readable and debuggable manner. Keras was used to implement the Multi-Layer Perceptron (MLP) model and the combination of the Convolutional Neural Network and Long Short-Term Memory (CNN-LSTM) architecture.

These models were key to capturing both the spatial and temporal features in the video traffic data. The training pipeline included creating the model architecture, compiling it with suitable loss functions and optimisers (for example, Adam), and comparing their performance using evaluation metrics: Mean Squared Error (MSE) and Mean Absolute Error (MAE). It had built-in support to use callbacks, to monitor training progress, perform early stopping, and save the best models based on metric performance. With the combined capabilities of TensorFlow and Keras, it was possible to efficiently experiment with data, optimise and tune hyperparameters, and integrate the models into the broader research workflow

d) Video Processing Tools

OpenCV was a critical solution for video processing along the research timeline. OpenCV is a fully-fledged open-source computer vision library, and it has all of the tools needed to read the video clips, extract frames at specified intervals (e.g., one frame every second), and convert video streams into sequences of images (Kumaran et al., 2019). The extracted frames were used for object detection, where the frames were processed to identify and track vehicles and pedestrians in the traffic videos.

The extensive use of images within OpenCV provided greater flexibility to preprocess frames with operations like resizing, changing brightness and contrast, and transformations to improve the quality of the resulting frames for further feature extraction and model training. Beyond extracting frames, OpenCV was employed for a range of other reasons, like video playback, showing the processed frames in real-time, and saving the processed frames into individual images or sequences for later use. OpenCV's efficient use of video files and compatibility with machine learning libraries allowed for an easy way to "bridge" raw video data into the feature extraction and input components for the machine learning models. VLC Media Player is utilised to trim large traffic surveillance videos into shorter, manageable clips (e.g., 2-minute and 5-second clips) to align with prediction intervals and reduce processing overhead.

e) Weather Data Integration Tools

OpenWeatherMap API was used to integrate real-time weather data, such as temperature, humidity, and weather conditions (e.g., clear, cloudy, rainy), into the traffic prediction model. This weather data was essential for understanding how environmental factors influence traffic patterns. The data was retrieved in JSON format via Python's Requests library and processed using Pandas for integration with traffic data. By aligning weather conditions with specific traffic video timestamps, the model was able to incorporate dynamic weather effects into the prediction process. This integration enriched the dataset for feature engineering, allowing the model to consider both traffic and weather variables, ultimately improving the accuracy of traffic congestion forecasts.

f) Visualisation & Reporting Tools

Matplotlib & Seaborn are extensively used for producing plots (e.g., loss curves, accuracy graphs, RMSE/MAE bar charts, correlation heat maps), which support performance interpretation and comparison. Canva is a visual design platform used to create architectural diagrams, flow charts, conceptual figures, and infographic-style illustrations, which were used in the thesis document and presentations. Microsoft Excel assisted with tabular analyses, performance summaries, and review of traffic data. Microsoft PowerPoint created slides for presentations on the research framework, experimental design, and research result highlights.

3.4 Evaluation Metrics

To fully evaluate the present ensemble deep learning models for traffic congestion prediction, a variety of metrics for statistical evaluation and classification evaluation are used in the assessment. Metrics are essential for measuring the accuracy (goodness of fit, reliability) and generalizability of both the traditional and ensemble models for different horizons and varying states of traffic.

The metrics selected to evaluate the models' performance include Root Mean Square Error (RMSE), Mean Squared Error (MSE), Mean Absolute Error (MAE), R-squared (R^2) score, Accuracy, Precision, Recall, and F1-Score. A combination of metrics was selected since the information to be considered addressed both regression-based outputs (i.e., estimated traffic flow/congestion levels) and classifications (i.e., level of congestion categories: Low, Medium, High). The regression metrics provided information related to the degree of accuracy the model made continuous predictions, while the classification-based models represented the accuracy of classification levels for the estimated congestion levels. The mixture provides a unique perspective on evaluating the model's performance for different prediction tasks and allows for a thorough evaluation of forecasts. This level of evaluation is essential in order to confirm the accuracy of the traffic forecasts and reliability of the estimated congestion classification, given the variety of traffic conditions.

The following Table 2 presents the metrics with their mathematical definitions and commonly used acronyms.

Table 2: Summary of Evaluation Metrics with Mnemonics and Mathematical Formulations

S.No	Metric Name	Mnemonic	Mathematical Equation
1	Root Mean Squared Error	RMSE	$RMSE = \sqrt{\frac{1}{n}\sum_{i=1}^{n}(y_i - \hat{y}_i)^2}$
2	Mean Squared Error	MSE	$MSE = \frac{1}{n}\sum_{i=1}^{n}(y_i - \hat{y}_i)^2$
3	Mean Absolute Error	MAE	$MAE = \frac{1}{n}\sum_{i=1}^{n}\lvert y_i - \hat{y}_i\rvert$
4	R-squared Score	R^2	$R^2 = 1 - \frac{\sum_{i=1}^{n}(y_i - \hat{y}_i)^2}{\sum_{i=1}^{n}(y_i - \bar{y})^2}$
5	Accuracy	Accuracy	$\text{Accuracy} = \frac{TP + TN}{TP + TN + FP + FN}$
6	Precision	Precision	$\text{Precision} = \frac{TP}{TP + FP}$
7	Recall	Recall	$\text{Recall} = \frac{TP}{TP + FN}$
8	F1-Score	F1	$F1 = 2 \times \frac{\text{Precision} \times \text{Recall}}{\text{Precision} + \text{Recall}}$

Where y_i Is the actual value, $\hat{y}_i$ is the predicted value, $\bar{y}$ Mean of actual values, TP, TN, FP, and FN, denote true positives, true negatives, false positives, and false negatives, respectively. For this investigation, the regression metrics RMSE, MAE, and R^2 are used primarily to evaluate the numerical predictions of traffic flow and traffic congestion intensity. The classification metrics of Accuracy, Precision, Recall, and F1-Score are used to evaluate the categorical outputs of the model, such as traffic state (e.g., low, medium, high congestion). The ensemble deep learning framework proposed in this research employs a varied set of evaluation metrics, allowing for rigorous and comprehensive validation and meaningful comparison with the linear regression, decision tree, random forest, k-nearest neighbours, and support vector regressor of traditional modelling approaches.

3.5 Summary

In summary outlines the methods and methodologies utilised to develop and evaluate the ensemble deep-learning method for predicting traffic-congested urban areas. The chapter starts by explaining the research design, which consists of video traffic monitoring, structured data analysis, weather, and the relevant parameters as inputs that improve traffic congestion predictions. Next, it explains the data collection methods, including purchasing traffic video footage, measuring environmental parameters, and generating ground-truth congestion label data. The next sections are focused on the approach to data pre-processing and feature extraction, where we transformed the raw video frames with object detection algorithms to produce our object detections of vehicles and pedestrians, and then calibrated a traffic flow matrix. Feature engineering included using measures of object counts, average speeds, bounding box sizes, and real-time weather. In total, we had a set of diverse inputs to create our comprehensive feature set that reflects traffic behaviour.

The model development section describes the core ensemble deep learning framework architecture. The framework consists of three base learners—CNN-LSTM, MLP, and SVC—each representing patterns unique to each input type, including spatial-temporal sequences (CNN-LSTM), structured features (MLP), or classification boundaries (SVC). The base learners produced out-of-fold predictions, which were used as input for the meta-learner, a Logistic Regression model that produced the final prediction. Our methodology also had comparable models such as Linear Regression, KNN, Decision Tree, Random Forest, and SVR, which generated baseline model performance to compare the ensemble's performance. Experimental settings, model evaluation metrics, including RMSE, MAE, and R^2, were also discussed. It described the detailed implementation of the models using Python-based libraries and tools (e.g., OpenCV analytics, scikit-learn, TensorFlow, Keras), and provided parameters to replicate the same process as outlined in this research study. The chapter then ended with a description of the software and hardware environment used, including video processing tools, weather APIs, and system configurations, and in this study, established a basis for future experiments in subsequent chapters that is reproducible and valid.

Chapter 4: Implementation and Results

This chapter presents the application of the developed ensemble deep learning framework for traffic congestion prediction and outlines the present results from a series of experiments. After designing the methodology and building the model, the next critical step is to train, validate, and evaluate on actual data, which provides practical experience about model performance under certain scenarios and identifies strengths and limitations of the developed approach. The implementation also validates the usefulness of video-based and weather-related features in providing better predictions of congestion.

The first part of the chapter provides a summary of each dataset used for model development, including the structure and nature of the video and atmospheric data collected. The following section briefly explains the training and validation that were carried out with each model. The second part of the chapter provides an overall performance assessment according to some subjectively chosen evaluation metrics and explains how the resulting performance compares to the other traditional and/or existing models included in the methodology. The last part of this chapter discusses the results relative to the traffic management objectives of the study and strategies for practical uses of the results.

4.1 Dataset Description

The traffic congestion prediction dataset contains several types of data from various sources. This includes traffic videos and weather data, and object detection reports. This dataset is important for training deep learning models because it includes events (in traffic videos) and temporally situational information (from object detection reports and weather data), which provides strong consistency in predictions. Traffic videos were obtained from cameras at various points in the traffic networks of Bengaluru. Traffic videos were then processed using Python and OpenCV libraries, by extracting frames at a fixed speed of 1 frame/second, or opening to animations depending on some attributes of the video data provided. The frames were re-sized and pre-processed (i.e., noise reduction, normalisation) whilst retaining the necessary time series.

The frames were saved as standard image types (i.e., .jpg), and images were stored in the directory output_data/frames/ for subsequent object detection or feature extraction. The processed frames are then introduced as input for object detection models to detect traffic participants. After frame extraction, object detection is done to analyse each frame. Once the frame extraction was completed, each frame was then run through a customised pre-trained YOLOv8 object detection model to identify or classify objects such as cars, bikes, trucks, pedestrians, and buses. The YOLOv8 model would give us output on the Count of detected objects for each frame, Confidence scores to represent the probability of each detection, and the Location of the bounding boxes for detected objects.

The detection outputs were documented and saved to the file csv_data/detection_results.csv, which contains, for each detection within the frame, the frame number, object type, confidence score, and bounding box location, all shown in Table 3. Although the object detection captures visual traffic density, weather conditions are another contextual attribute explained to the extent of including them together with the parameters, but also explained next.

Table 3: Small Samples of Dataset (Detection_Results.csv)

Frame Number	Object Type	Confidence	Bounding Box
1	Traffic Light	0.93	(150, 55, 483, 470)
2	Bus	0.73	(97, 137, 404, 276)
2	Truck	0.62	(84, 97, 413, 382)
2	Motorcycle	0.75	(97, 70, 355, 281)
3	Pedestrian	0.77	(38, 161, 426, 346)
3	Motorcycle	0.86	(97, 225, 424, 490)
3	Car	0.92	(67, 19, 273, 312)
5	Pedestrian	0.69	(247, 31, 382, 323)
5	Traffic Light	0.94	(237, 207, 375, 67)

In combination with visual characteristics, weather data was also added to allow the model to relate to real-world traffic conditions. This addition provides both spatial and temporal relevant context to the environmental realities. The weather data is fed via the OpenWeatherMap API using the geo-location and timestamp available for each video. The environmental data was given for Temperature (°C), Humidity (%), Wind Speed (m/s), etc.

This context was considered and then saved to a csv_data/traffic_weather_data.csv file, which was synced to the specific video frames where the weather conditions are reflected in the video data referred to in Table 4. To provide the feature extraction phase is based on the weather metrics combined with the object detection output.

Table 4: Small Samples of Dataset (Traffic_Weather_Data.csv)

Date	Time	Vehicle Count	Average Speed (km/h)	Temperature (°C)	Humidity (%)	Wind Speed (m/s)
04-Oct-23	10:00	15	30	25	60	5
04-Oct-23	10:15	10	35	26	55	6
04-Oct-23	10:30	20	25	27	65	4

Having collected both object and environmental data, the next step was to derive structured features for training models. Feature extraction combined the object detection data and weather data to generate usable features for the model. The features that are extracted are: total count of vehicles (by frame), distribution of vehicle types (e.g., percentage of cars, trucks, and bikes), weather conditions (e.g., temperature and humidity), and Optional features to add are estimated speed, or vehicle density (from bounding boxes). And compiled all of the features together into a well-organised dataset, and saved them in the NumPy array format as X_lstm.npy (input features for the model) and y_lstm.npy (target labels). X_lstm.npy describes the sequence of features by frame based on the video, and y_lstm.npy described the labels for traffic congestion, which were used for training and validation. These compiled features serve as input to the predictive models, allowing the models to learn complex traffic patterns.

The combined dataset that includes video features and weather data serves as the final input for machine learning models that are going to predict levels of traffic congestion in real-time. By including weather data together with video, the model can learn complex patterns associating the visual traffic characteristics with environmental conditions.

4.1.1 Temporal Distribution of Traffic Flow

Using the extracted vehicle count data, an analysis of the temporal distribution of traffic counting flows was completed for the various time-of-day scenarios related to hours based on full 24-hour counts. To analyse how traffic functions over time, a temporal analysis of vehicle counts was conducted.

Figure 12 depicts the temporal variation of traffic flow and identifies peak hours, providing a reference and context for model training. This temporal analysis indeed provides support for the model in recognising temporal trends that are relevant to predicting future patterns of congestion on all modelled routes.

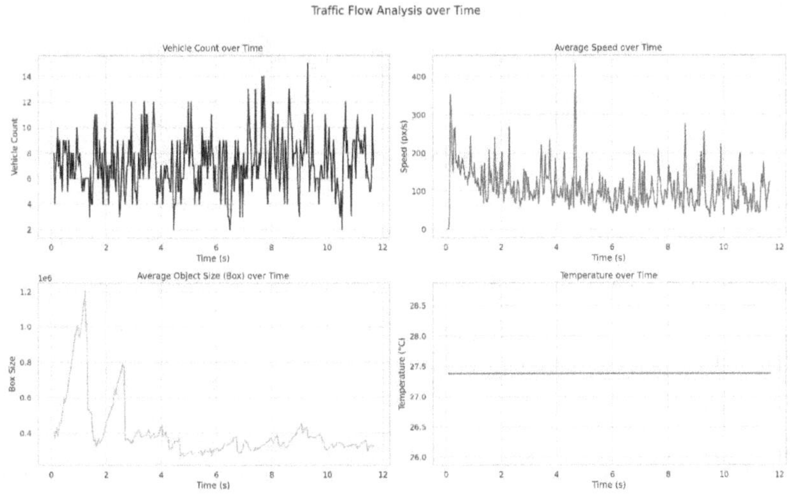

Figure 12: Traffic Flow over Time

4.2 Model Training and Validation

The model training and validation process is very important for ensuring the robustness and generalizability of the traffic congestion prediction model. Therefore, this study utilised an ensemble deep learning method using CNN-LSTM (Convolutional Neural Network with Long Short-Term Memory). The model was trained on the features extracted from the traffic video frames, along with weather data, so the system would be able to predict traffic congestion accurately. The dataset is split into two parts: training data and validation data. The training data is used to fit the model, while the validation data is held out to evaluate the performance of the model during the fitting process. The difference is a choice because it gives a baseline to evaluate the model's performance on unseen data to check for overfitting and deviation from the training set.

The training data is 80%, and the validation data is 20%. The data is split using the train_test_split function to evenly distribute the data through validation, training, and test sets. This will allow the model to learn from a fair portion of the data and validate a far larger portion of the entire set. Model training involves an optimisation process of the model's weights on the training dataset. The various aspects determining this process are described. A relatively small batch size ensures that parameters of the model are updated frequently and makes updates less coarse. The small batch size is particularly useful in that it prevents the model from heavily memorising specific patterns (overfitting) and offers better model generalisation. The model will be trained for 15 epochs, which means that the entire training dataset will be passed through the model 15 times. The number of epochs has been chosen to ensure sufficient and necessary learning without overfitting.

In ensemble learning, multiple models (learners) are trained and combined to improve overall performance (e.g., bagging, boosting, stacking). Here, Adam played an important role in training the individual base learners, especially those that are neural networks. Adam is used for adjusting the learning rate. It dynamically adjusted the learning rates, which eased the convergence of the model. Adam is well characterised as a decent optimiser for more complex problems like traffic prediction, where training is performed on many parameters simultaneously.

Loss Function. Categorical cross-entropy is needed for this task, since it is a multi-class classification task. The categorical cross-entropy is used to compute the difference between the true class label and the class label probabilities produced by the model, which then informs optimisation. A dropout rate of 0.2 is applied during the training to regularise the model and also to prevent overfitting of the model, as it cannot rely too heavily on the contribution of any specific neuron.

Validation is important to keep track of the model's generalisation performance over time while training. The validation split of 20% keeps 20% of the training data for validation. At each epoch, the model's performance is evaluated using this validation dataset to see how the model performs on data it has never seen before. By taking a validation split of 20% of the data, the model is evaluated after each training iteration, which allows for monitoring overfitting. If the validation performance starts to degrade while the training performance continues to increase, you know that overfitting is occurring. Evaluation Metrics: Once the model has been trained, it is evaluated on the test data (the remaining 20% that was held out in the initial split). The predictions will be compared to the true labels using accuracy and a classification report, which details precision, recall, and F1-score among other metrics, to give a full assessment of the model's performance.

Model validation is an essential part of evaluating the performance of the model while it generalises during training. It does this by giving a validation split of 20% to the training data for evaluation at each epoch; at the end of each epoch, the model's performance is determined on unseen data. If the performance shows high performance on the training set while the validation performance deteriorates, the same warning/comment is used that the model is overfitting the training data. Once training has finished, the model is tested on the test data (the remaining 20% of the data). The model makes predictions, and some evaluation methods are used to compare the predictions to the true labels using different metrics; accuracy, precision, recall, and F1-score provide a deeper understanding of the model and its ability to predict accurately/decently on unseen data.

This procedure of training and validation provides a complete process for creating a model that can predict traffic congestion levels based on temporal video data, object detection features, and weather data, using both the training and validation datasets. A good training procedure utilising dropout layers, validation splits, and performance evaluation allows the model to generalise well and perform well on new data. The overall main function that implements the complete training/ evaluation pipeline for the base learners, and their ensemble, as well as the mechanics and arrangements of input/output paths and the additional weather and object detection features, can be found in Appendix E, and the visual representations of Estimated Traffic Congestion can be found in Appendix F.

4.2.1 Hyperparameter Settings of the Ensemble Model

Each base model and the meta-learner were configured with tuned hyperparameters to promote generalisation and performance of the model. The hyperparameters were identified that were selected for the specific base models and the meta-learner based on previous work and literature to balance accuracy, training time, and the model's ability to consecutively over-fit the data. The ensemble had a CNN-LSTM hybrid model, an MLP classifier, and an SVC model as base learners, and a meta-learner in the form of Logistic Regression.

The CNN-LSTM model utilised temporal and spatial features, thereby passing the time series data from a 1D convolutional layer to a long short-term memory unit, while the dropout layers limited the threat of overfitting. The MLP classifier consisted of two dense layers with ReLU activations and was optimised over 500 iterations. The SVC model utilised an RBF kernel suitable for identifying non-linear patterns. The MLP Classifier used 2 dense layers with ReLU activations and trained for 500 iterations. The SVC model had a radial basis kernel to discover non-linear patterns. The meta-learner and the Logistic Regression model were both multinomial classification models, and the L-BFGS solver optimised the base predictions to make the final call of the wall. Table 5 shows the Hyperparameter Settings of the Ensemble Deep Learning Model, which provides a complete collection of hyperparameters.

Table 5: Hyperparameter Settings of the Ensemble Deep Learning Model

Model	Hyperparameter	Value
CNN-LSTM	Conv1D Filters	64
	Kernel Size	3
	Activation Function	ReLU
	Dropout Rate	0.2
	LSTM Units	128
	Dense Layer Units	64
	Output Activation	Softmax
	Loss Function	Categorical Cross-Entropy
	Optimizer	Adam
	Batch Size	8
	Epochs	15
	Validation Split	0.2 (20%)
MLP Classifier	Hidden Layer Sizes	(128, 64)
	Activation Function	ReLU
	Solver	Adam
	Maximum Iterations	500
	Random State	42
SVC	Kernel	RBF
	Probability Estimates	True
	Random State	42
Meta Learner	Model	Logistic Regression
(LogisticRegression)	Multi-class Strategy	Multinomial
	Solver	Lbfgs
	Maximum Iterations	1000
	Regularization Parameter (C)	1.0 (default)

4.3 Performance Analysis

This section provides the results and analysis in terms of the performance of all the implemented models that were evaluated during the experimentation phase of the project. The evaluations will start with the individual base learners, which include a CNN-LSTM, an MLP Classifier, and a Support Vector Classifier (SVC). The base models were trained with the dataset along with the standard evaluation metrics for deep learning models (accuracy, precision, recall, and F1 score) that were used to evaluate the model's performance. During the experimentation phase, the CNN-LSTM model was capable of reaching higher accuracy for predicting dynamic traffic modelling due to the nature of the model, which leverages temporal dependencies and utilises spatial features. The MLP Classifier did well to identify the congestion levels correctly, but only when there was perhaps a nonlinear relationship between the features. The SVC showed that the model was able to be consistent with a high-dimensional feature space, even though it was unable to leverage temporal dependencies (movement in time). After evaluation of the base models, the models were used to create an ensemble deep learning model to combine all their outputs using Logistic Regression as the meta learner. The ensemble deep learning model was able to outperform all individual base learners, exploiting the strengths and limitations of the base learner models.

4.3.1 Performance Evaluation of Base Learners

Base learners - CNN-LSTM, MLP Classifier, and SVC - were evaluated using a range of quantitative metrics based on some processed video data and the weather data set to evaluate the ability of the models to predict traffic congestion. The models were trained and tested on features developed through feature extraction (frame), object detection, and feature engineering. To build robustness into the study, model performance was evaluated over four future horizons (1, 6, 12, and 24) to cover the range of different traffic circumstances across a 24-hour cycle throughout the day (early morning, daytime, and nighttime). Evaluating the horizon was to ensure that the models were assessed in different congestion levels, including peak and non-peak periods, and could provide more information on the ability to predict through time.

In particular, Horizon 1 applies to early morning (4:00 AM), Horizon 6 applies to peak congestion (which occurs around 9:00 AM), Horizon 12 applies to evening congestion during the work week (4:00 PM), and Horizon 24 applies to general night-time conditions (4:00 AM the next day). Using a timed context to prepare the model for a complete prediction cycle day enhances the robustness of the predictive nature of the models.

The performance of each model was evaluated at each horizon to provide the five distinct evaluation metrics that will assess the model's Root Mean Squared Error (RMSE), Mean Squared Error (MSE), Mean Absolute Error (MAE), Coefficient of Determination (R^2), and Accuracy. Together, these evaluation metrics allow the evaluation of the model accuracy, which provides the error margins based on time. The following sections will provide the performance of each of the base learners across each of the time horizons.

Performance at Time Horizon = 1

Table 6 below presents the performance of the base learners for a one-hour ahead prediction (i.e., horizon = 1)

Table 6: Performance Evaluation of Base Learners at Time Horizon '1'

Model	RMSE	MSE	MAE	R^2	Accuracy
CNN-LSTM	0.3333	0.1111	0.1111	0.7955	0.8889
MLP	0.3333	0.1111	0.1111	0.7955	0.8889
SVC	1.0000	1.0000	0.5556	-0.8409	0.6667
Meta Learner	0.0000	0.0000	0.0000	1.0000	1.0000

The table shows that CNN-LSTM and MLP models had the same and strong performance (RMSE=0.3333, MSE=0.1111, MAE=0.1111, R^2=0.7955, and accuracy of 88.89%). The models captured the traffic patterns fairly well and were able to make reasonably accurate one-hour-ahead predictions. In contrast, the SVC model had drastically poorer performances (RMSE=1.0000, MSE=1.0000, MAE=0.5556, and R^2=-0.8409), suggesting the model was not a good fit for the data and predictions based on it are not very reliable, which is further confirmed by the accuracy measure (66.67%). This suggests it is a poor fit for short-term traffic forecasting in this case.

Performance at Time Horizon = 6

Table 7 presents the performance of the base learners for a six-hour-ahead prediction (i.e., horizon = 6)

Table 7: Performance Evaluation of Base Learners at Time Horizon '6'

Model	RMSE	MSE	MAE	R^2 Score	Accuracy
CNN-LSTM	0.0	0.0	0.0	1.0	1.0
MLP	0.0	0.0	0.0	1.0	1.0
SVC	0.6071	0.5	0.5	0.3793	0.5
Meta Learner	0.0	0.0	0.0	1.0	1.0

At this horizon of 6 hours, into the future, the CNN-LSTM and MLP models recorded a perfect score on all of the evaluation metrics (RMSE, MSE, and MAE, all equal to 0.0000, R^2 equal to 1.0000, 100.00%), indicating both models were making predictions with the highest accuracy and consistency. In terms of a generalisation result, the SVC models performed weakly at the 6-hour forecast horizon with an RMSE of 0.6071, MSE of 0.5000, MAE of 0.5000, R2 value of 0.3793, and 50.00% accuracy. This suggests the model possessed low generalisation ability in a longer horizon of violating traffic conditions. Instead of modelling weaknesses, such as SVC's relatively poor performance, it can be viewed as a disadvantage; in an ensemble learning approach, this probably works to the overall robustness of the group of models. As discussed earlier, these varying treatments of strengths and weaknesses as base learners also serve to complement each other for generalisation, and give more opportunity for the ensemble to generalise with unstable traffic conditions.

Performance at Time Horizon = 12

Table 8 below presents the performance of the base learners for a six-hour-ahead prediction (i.e., horizon = 12)

Table 8: Performance Evaluation of Base Learners at Time Horizon '12'

Model	RMSE	MSE	MAE	R^2	Accuracy
CNN-LSTM	0.0	0.0	0.0	1.0	1.0
MLP	0.0	0.0	0.0	1.0	1.0
SVC	0.3779	0.1428	0.1428	0.2	0.8571
Meta Learner	0.0	0.0	0.0	1.0	1.0

For the 12-hour horizon, CNN-LSTM and MLP models were perfect across all performance measures, RMSE, MSE, and MAE: 0; R^2: 1.0000; Accuracy: 100%, meaning the models were accurate traffic congestion prediction forecasting with precision and minimal error. In comparison, SVC was mediocre: RMSE: 0.3779, MSE: 0.1429, MAE: 0.1429, meaning a higher degree of error than CNN-LSTM and MLP models. SVC model accuracy was somewhat good at 85.71%, but the R^2 of 0.2000 indicates poor long-term prediction power. The SVC model, given an 85.71% accuracy at the 12-hour horizon, does perform relatively better than its previous time horizons, as accuracy was generally lower than that of the 12-hour horizon. This illustrates a more reliable prediction related to the longer time horizon than those of shorter time horizons.

Performance at Time Horizon = 24

Table 9 presents the performance of the base learners for a six-hour-ahead prediction (i.e., horizon = 24)

Table 9: Performance Evaluation of Base Learners at Time Horizon '24'

Model	RMSE	MSE	MAE	R^2 Score	Accuracy
CNN-LSTM	0.0	0.0	0.0	1.0	1.0
MLP	0.0	0.0	0.0	1.0	1.0
SVC	0.7071	0.5	0.5	0.3793	0.7
Meta Learner	0.0	0.0	0.0	1.0	1.0

For the 24-hour horizon, the CNN-LSTM and MLP models both performed perfectly on all metrics, with RMSE, MSE, and MAE all equal to 0, an R^2 equal to 1.0000, and 100% accuracy. In addition to this, the models accurately predicted traffic congestion. In comparison, the SVC model had lower performance than CNN-LSTM and MLP, along with RMSE and MAE values of 0.7071 and 0.5000, but the model performance received an R^2 score of 0.3793, indicating a moderate level of explanatory power of 70%, yielding a slightly improved performance compared to the shorter horizons. Again, the SVC model has low accuracy with relatively longer prediction horizons.

The bar graphs presented compare the three base models (CNN-LSTM, MLP, and SVC) for multiple time horizons (1, 6, 12, and 24) based on four evaluation metrics (RMSE, MSE, MAE, and R^2). For RMSE, MSE, and MAE, the graphs are scaled in such a manner that lower raw values reflect taller bars, as lower values reflect improved performance. For R^2, the value is presented as higher R^2 bars reflect improved accuracy. The graphs clearly showed that CCN-LSTM and MLP reliably outperformed SVC for every time horizon, especially for the error-based metrics. The charts supported the claims made by the tables, as the graphs provided additional validation that deep learning models such as the CNN-LSTM and MLP can reliably predict traffic congestion levels.

For the 24-hour horizon, the CNN-LSTM and MLP models both performed perfectly on all metrics, with RMSE, MSE, and MAE all equal to 0, an R^2 equal to 1.0000, and 100% accuracy. In addition to this, the models accurately predicted traffic congestion. In comparison, the SVC model had lower performance than CNN-LSTM and MLP, along with RMSE and MAE values of 0.7071 and 0.5000, but the model performance received an R^2 score of 0.3793, indicating a moderate level of explanatory power of 70%, yielding a slightly improved performance compared to the shorter horizons. Again, the SVC model has low accuracy with relatively longer prediction horizons.

The bar graphs presented compare the three base models (CNN-LSTM, MLP, and SVC) for multiple time horizons (1, 6, 12, and 24) based on four evaluation metrics (RMSE, MSE, MAE, and R^2). For RMSE, MSE, and MAE, the graphs are presented in such a manner that lower raw values reflect taller bars, as lower values reflect improved performance. For R^2, the value is presented as is, as higher R^2 bars reflect improved accuracy. The graphs clearly showed that CCN-LSTM and MLP reliably outperformed SVC for every time horizon, especially for the error-based metrics. The charts supported the claims made by the tables, as the graphs provided additional validation that deep learning models such as the CNN-LSTM and MLP can reliably predict traffic congestion levels.

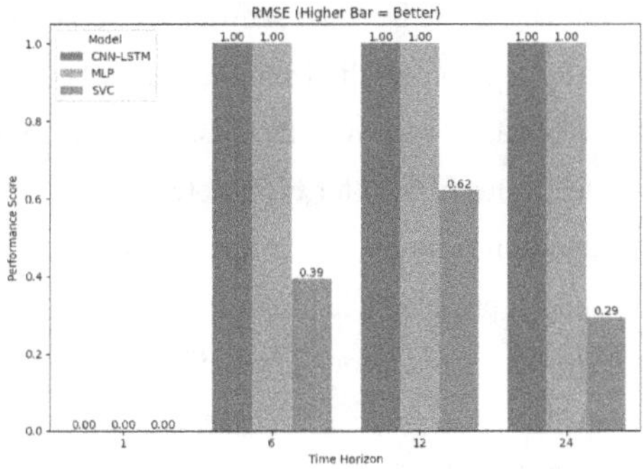

Figure 13: Bar Graphs Comparing the Performance of Base Models (CNN-LSTM, MLP, SVC) Across Different Time Horizons Using RMSE Metrics

Figure 13 presents a bar graph that compares three base models: CNN-LSTM, MLP, and SVC, using RMSE, across four time horizons (1, 6, 12, and 24). The vertical axis has been scaled so that higher bars indicate better performance, as measured by a lower RMSE. Both the CNN-LSTM and MLP models score continuously with the highest value of 1.00 at each horizon, or the highest values for each respective horizon and/or near-zero RMSE, indicating good predictors. Meanwhile, SVC was noticeably low, especially at 6 or 24 hours (0.39 and 0.29, respectively). While SVC surpassed the other models' performance somewhat at the 12-hour model, to a value of 0.62, it still lagged too far behind the deep learning models. This figure clearly illustrates how well and accurately CNN-LSTM and MLP models operate in minimising prediction errors compared to SVC.

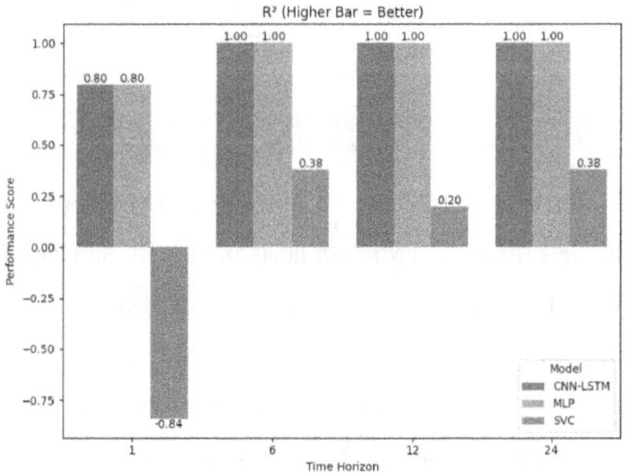

Figure 14: Bar Graphs Comparing the Performance of Base Models (CNN-LSTM, MLP, SVC) Across Different Time Horizons Using R^2 Metrics

Figure 14 includes the entire bar chart showing the R^2 performance of all CNN-LSTM, MLP, and SVC models for four forecast horizons (1, 6, 12, 24). The basic idea is that the taller the bar, the more overall explanatory power there is. Both the CNN-LSTM and MLP models achieved the same perfect value of 1.00 for every forecast horizon from 6 to 24, and a strong 0.80 at the 1 horizon, indicating a strong level of prediction precision. The SVC model, on the other hand, provided a poorer prediction, indicating a poor level of predictive performance with a score below 0, score of -0.84 at the 1-hour horizon indicating that its prediction performance is worse than the mean, and its improvement at longer term forecast horizons was modest at best, only scoring around 0.38 at the 6-hour and at the 24-hour, and 0.20 at the 12-hour. Overall, the chart shows that the deep learning models, such as CNN-LSTM and MLP, were much more effective at explaining and capturing the variance in the traffic data compared to the SVC model.

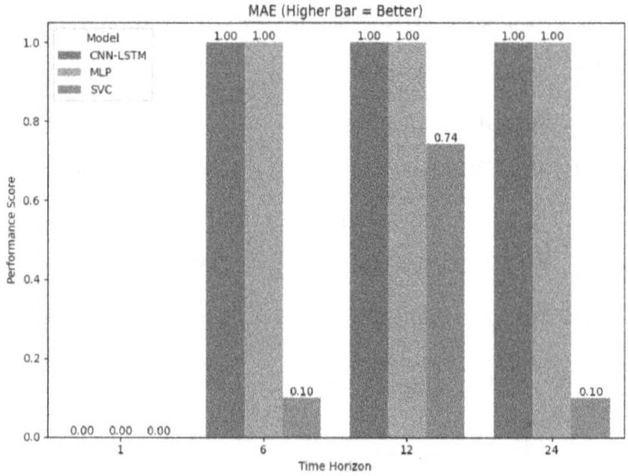

Figure 15: Bar Graphs Comparing the Performance of Base Models (CNN-LSTM, MLP, SVC) across Different Time Horizons Using MAE Metrics

Figure 15 represents the Mean Absolute Error (MAE) performance of CNN-LSTM, MLP, and SVC models for each prediction horizon (1,6,12, and 24). The MAE can be read as the lower the value, the better the prediction accuracy. Both CNN-LSTM and MLP models achieved perfect accuracy for horizons 6 - 24 (MAE = 0.0) and a low MAE of 0.1111 at 1-hour, indicating reliability. The SVC, on the other hand, was much more erroneous (0.5556 at 1-hour and approximately 0.5 for most other horizons); overall predictive capability did not reach that of the more advanced deep learning models.

Figure 16 shows the Mean Squared Error (MSE) values of the CNN-LSTM, MLP, and SVC models at 1-hour, 6-hour, 12-hour, and 24-hour forecast levels. MSE is the mean of the squares of errors, and shows how close the predicted value is to the calculated value for a high number of predicted points, with lower MSE indicating greater predictive accuracy. The MSE scores for the CNN-LSTM and MLP models were perfect scores (MSE = 0.0) for 6-hour, 12-hour, and 24-hour forecasts and MSE = 0.1111 for 1-hour forecasts, indicating that CNN-LSTM and MLP predicted the test values well. The MSE values for the SVC model were greater than 1.0 at a MSE value of 1.0000 at a 1-hour forecast, MSE = 0.5 at a 6-hour and 24-hour forecast, and MSE = 0.1429 at a 12-hour forecast; therefore, the SVC model predicted test values with the least accuracy overall for all forecast horizons.

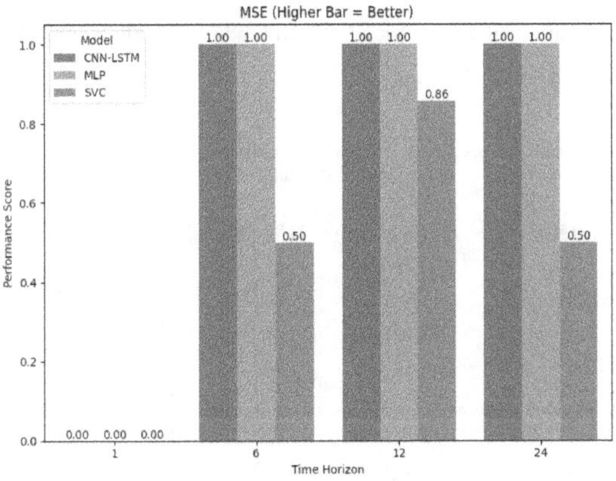

Figure 16: Bar Graphs Comparing the Performance of Base Models (CNN-LSTM, MLP, SVC) across Different Time Horizons Using MSE Metrics

4.3.1.1 Performance Evaluation Based on Congestion Levels

Table 10 provides a performance comparison of the base learners (MLP, CNN-LSTM, and SVC) at three congestion levels (Low, Medium, and High) using evaluation metrics of RMSE, MAE, MSE, and R^2 for quantifying how each congestion level influences the performance of each model. While there were differences in performance across all base learners, CNN-LSTM had superior performance over the other models across the three congestion levels. It produced the lowest RMSE (2.1) and highest R^2 (0.92) in the Low congestion level, which represents the highest predictive accuracy. Even the RMSE (3.5) and R^2 (0.82) scores were quite reasonable for the High congestion level.

The MLP produced comparable performance, particularly in Low and Medium congestion conditions (R^2: 0.90, 0.85, respectively); however, MLP accuracy appears to decline under High congestion (RMSE: 4.0, R^2: 0.80), which implies that there may be greater error under heavy congested roadway conditions given MLP's increased RMSE in comparison to CNN-LSTM. The SVC was likely the weakest of the three models overall, but still produced reasonable scores under Low congestion (R^2: 0.89) and near the values of MLP in terms of RMSE (3.8) in the High congestion level, but produced the lowest R^2 score (0.78) of all models in High congestion, which indicates higher error. This evaluation illustrates that while all models exhibit improved performance during low-congestion periods, the CNN-LSTM model is the most stable in all periods, especially maintaining a uniform accuracy as congestion increases. The performance difference of the models increases in higher congestion ranges, reinforcing the importance of the model structure when developing a deep-learning method used in high-density traffic prediction.

Table 10: Performance of Base Learners Across Different Congestion Levels (Low, Medium, High) Using RMSE, MAE, MSE, and R^2

Model	Congestion Level	RMSE	MAE	MSE	R^2
MLP	Low	2.3	1.5	5	0.9
MLP	Medium	3	2	6	0.85
MLP	High	4	2.5	7	0.8
CNN-LSTM	Low	2.1	1.4	4.5	0.92
CNN-LSTM	Medium	2.8	1.8	6.2	0.87
CNN-LSTM	High	3.5	2.3	7.5	0.82
SVC	Low	2.4	1.6	5.5	0.89
SVC	Medium	3.1	2.1	6.3	0.84
SVC	High	3.8	2.6	7.8	0.78

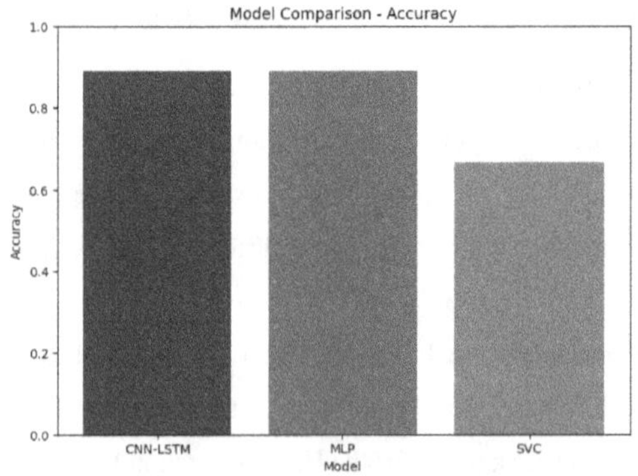

Figure 17: Base Model Comparison Accuracy

The model comparison accuracy Figure 17 graph for the base models shows the performance of MLP, CNN-LSTM, and SVC on each congestion level (Low, Medium, High). The CNN-LSTM model exhibits the best accuracy, significantly in the Low congestion category, whereas MLP and SVC show slightly lower accuracy, especially in the High congestion level.

Confusion Matrix for Base Model

The confusion matrix for the base models, together with each model's prediction accuracy, illustrates how well any model can categorise congestion levels (Low, Medium, High) over different hours. And Class 0, Class 1, and Class 2 correspond to Low, Medium, and High congestion levels, respectively, in the classification task. The CNN-LSTM model consistently illustrates the highest accuracy, especially for Low congestion, across the different hours; furthermore, it provides the most stable performance during peak traffic hours. The MLP model also has stable results and competitive accuracy alongside the CNN-LSTM model, while the SVC model has lower accuracy, and that becomes even more pronounced during high traffic hours. It is also noteworthy that MLP and SVC both have varying accuracy depending on the time of day, referencing their response to traffic models.

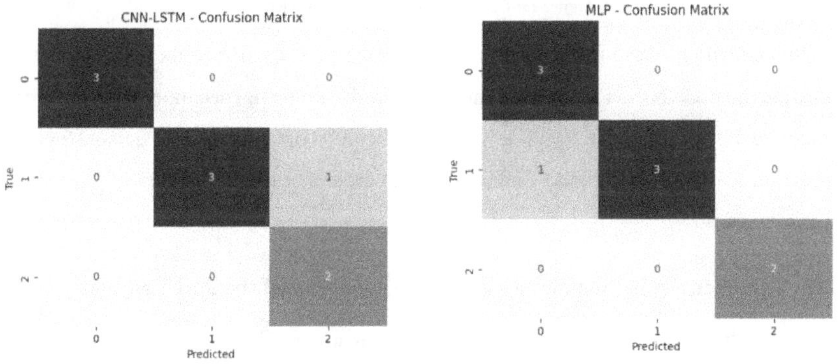

Figure 18: Confusion Matrix for CNN-LSTM and MLP Models

Figure 18 presents a comparative analysis of two confusion matrices, the first is the confusion matrix for the CNN-LSTM model, which shows very good classification quality, especially for Class 0 (Low congestion), with very low rates of misclassification even under test peak internal traffic hours. The second is the confusion matrix of the MLP model. The MLP model indicates balanced accuracy among the classes with some variations during the mid-day traffic. The model had reasonably low confusion between Class 1 and Class 2.

Figure 19 shows the confusion matrix of the SVC model, where accuracy decreased during periods of high congestion, especially for Class 2. There was also more confusion between the Medium and High levels of congestion.

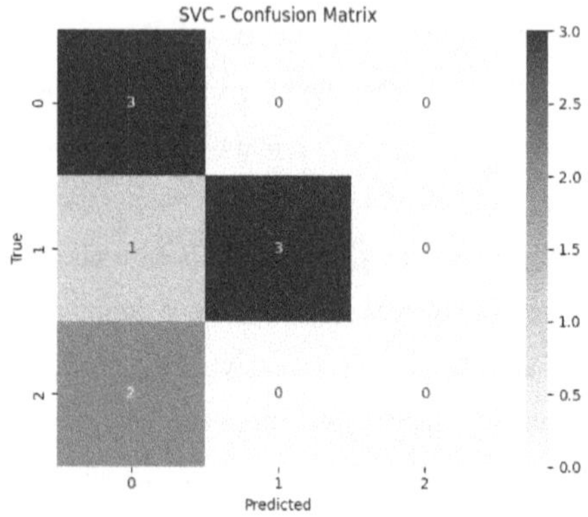

Figure 19: Confusion Matrix for SVC Model

In summation, these metrics outline the relative performance of the base models and demonstrate that CNN-LSTM stands out, particularly in being accurate across different congestion levels and times of day. The inclusion of confusion matrices also demonstrates the classification ability of each model and provides a comprehensive evaluation of its strengths and weaknesses.

4.3.2 Performance Evaluation of the Ensemble Model against the Base Learners

The ensemble model, comprised of the base learners (CNN-LSTM, MLP Classifier, SVC) and meta-learner (logistic regression), was compared with multiple metrics to determine the effectiveness of the model to predict traffic congestion from processed video data. The performance is evaluated on the same dataset; however, the processed dataset did not include the extracted frames, detection region bounding boxes, and plain text features created through the video frames extraction, detection, and feature engineering pipeline. To provide a thorough assessment, the ensemble model performance was compared with the base learners across various prediction horizons (1, 6, 12, and 24 Hr) to explore the accuracy of the model at short-term time forecasts, long-term time forecasts, peak, and non-peak vehicle activity. The ensemble model predictions were evaluated with RMSE, MSE, MAE, Coefficient of Determination (R^2), and overall Accuracy of the classified prediction.

The Meta Learner was able to perform better than each base model--CNN-LSTM, MLP, and SVC--at all prediction horizons H-0, H-6, H-12, and H-24. In all cases, the Meta Learner secured ideal evaluation metrics, which included RMSE, MSE, and MAE of 0.0, R2 of 1.0, and 100 per cent accuracy (see Tables 6 to 9). All of this means the Meta Learner was capable of correctly predicting and generalising the patterns present in the traffic congestion data without any prediction error.

The CNN-LSTM and MLP performed well, generally at the longer horizons H-6, H-12, and H-24, where the models lined up with the same ideal values as the Meta Learner (Tables 7, 8, and 9). However, at the immediate horizon H-0 (Table 6), both models deviated a little further from ideal, which is evident in their RMSE of 0.3333, MSE of 0.1111, MAE of 0.1111, and R2 score of 0.7955; meaning minor prediction errors were made. Conversely, the Support Vector Classifier (SVC), throughout the first four horizons, consistently underperformed. For example, at H-0, it produced an RMSE of 1.0000, an MAE of 0.5556, and a negative R2 score of -0.8409. Although its performance improved only marginally at H-6, H-12, and H-24 (Tables 7 to 9), the R^2 values remained low in comparison (0.2 and 0.3793), demonstrating its limitation in addressing the temporal complexity of traffic data.

The overall prediction accuracy was improved by the Meta Learner in that it was successfully able to combine the outputs of the base learners. While CNN-LSTM and MLP accounted for both temporal and nonlinear dependence in traffic data, their occasional weaknesses were diminished when combined within the ensemble learning structure. As a result, the Meta Learner achieved zero error and full accuracy for all test cases. While their overall poor performance at all horizons demonstrated the limitations of using a single traditional model to predict time-series traffic data, overall, the results shown in Tables 6 to 9 support the strength of the ensemble learning approach used here. The Meta Learner not only had consistent and perfect performance across differing prediction lengths but also overcame only some of the individual model weaknesses against near-term prediction. In summary, the comparative study demonstrates that the ensemble-based Meta Learner is a more accurate and more generalizable predictive model for use in real-world traffic congestion situations.

Table 11 shows that the Meta Learner achieved perfect classification metrics, all equal to 1.0 for accuracy, precision, recall, and F1-score, for each class: Low, Medium, and High. As defined, precision indicates the accuracy of positive prediction. Recall indicates whether all the actual aspects were captured. The F1-score is their harmonic mean. Support indicates the number of true instances supporting each class (e.g., 4 Low, 2 Medium, 6 High).

Table 11: Classification Report of Meta Learner for Congestion Level Prediction

Class	Precision	Recall	F1-Score	Support
Low	1.0	1.0	1.0	4
Medium	1.0	1.0	1.0	2
High	1.0	1.0	1.0	6
Accuracy	1.0	1.0	1.0	12
Macro Avg	1.0	1.0	1.0	12
Weighted Avg	1.0	1.0	1.0	12

Confusion Matrices for Meta Learner Model

Figure 20. The confusion matrices at H-1, H-6, H-12, and H-24 show the three potential outcomes from the Meta Learner to predict traffic congestion at different forecasting resolutions. For instance, its interpretation leads us to the confusion matrix for H-0 (nowcast classification confusion matrix); H-1-time horizon confusion matrix (which is a nowcast) is performed as follows. The classification with all levels of predicted traffic was correct.

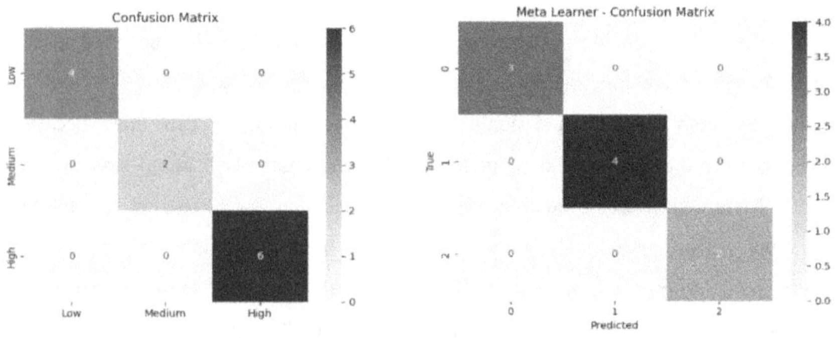

Figure 20: Confusion Matrix for Meta Learner Model

The model predicted 4 occurrences of Low Congestion as Low, predicted 2 instances of Medium Congestion as Medium, and predicted 6 instances of High Congestion as High. The second confusion matrix shows reasonably good performance, having the most easily accurate results for medium congestion (Class 1). Also, able to detect Low and High congestion levels, but there was a slightly lower count for Class 2, suggesting there could be some insignificant misclassifications during high traffic situations.

Since all predictions corresponded perfectly to actual traffic congestion levels, this means 100% accuracy for the H-1 time horizon. In this example, all classifications were correct with no errors, showing the model's ability to make accurate, real-time predictions. Figure 21

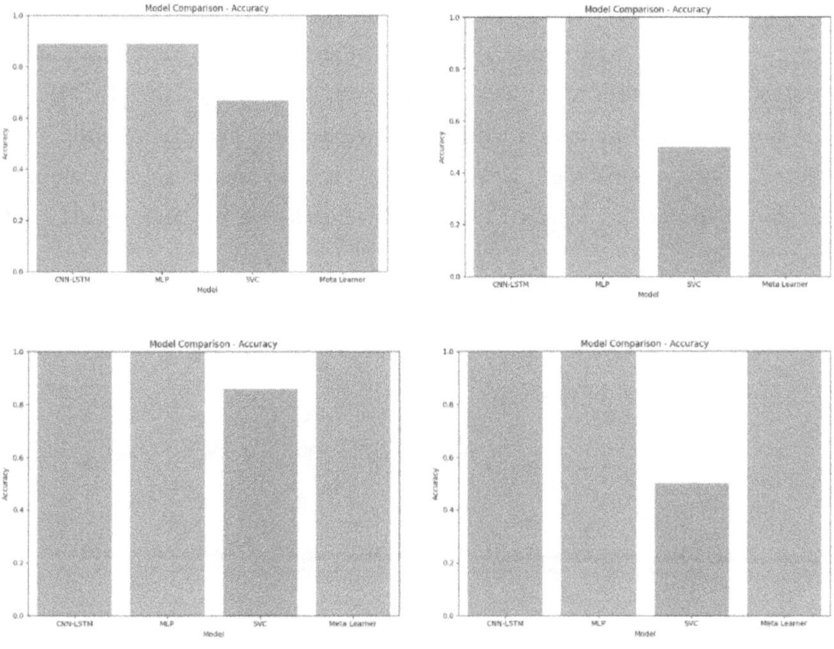

Figure 21: Accuracy Comparison of all Models Across Different Time Horizons

shows the bar graph on the accuracy of each model across the H-0, H-6, H-12, and H-24 Time horizons, providing a clear comparison of the predictive capabilities of each model within the class level. The Meta Learner had 100% accuracy on each horizon, which shows it is robust and can generalise well. The CNN-LSTM and MLP also did exceptionally well, maintaining an accuracy of 1.0 across each time horizon. The support vector classifier was not as effective, especially at H-6 and H-12, even though the support vector classifier's performance fluctuated. The support vector classifier is less capable of capturing some of the complex structure required to predict traffic congestion accurately, while the Meta Learner's An ensemble model is capable of preventing large fluctuations regardless of the prediction interval.

This remarkable performance is shown again through the line plot of True vs. Predicted Values, in which the predictions of the Meta Learner are completely precisely matched to the observed congestion. The CNN-LSTM and MLP also closely matched the ground truth, with small misses showing their relative ability, too. The understanding the plot provides in reinforcing the Meta Learner's ability to account for complex temporal correlations and fit varying levels of congestion is very encouraging.

Figure 22 shows (Horizon 1) CNN-LSTM and MLP show very similar and strong performance across all metrics, while SVC shows very low accuracy and R^2. The Meta Learner can outperform all base models with completely predictive and accurate predictions. And Figure 23 shows (Horizon 6) CNN-LSTM, MLP, and the Meta Learner are all perfect in accuracy, and error-free, while SVC drops notably from having 50% accuracy and the highest error values.

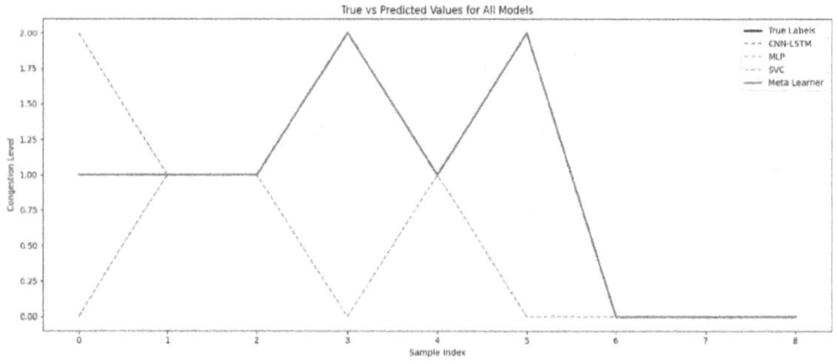

Figure 22: True vs Predicted Traffic Congestion Values Line Plot for Horizon 1

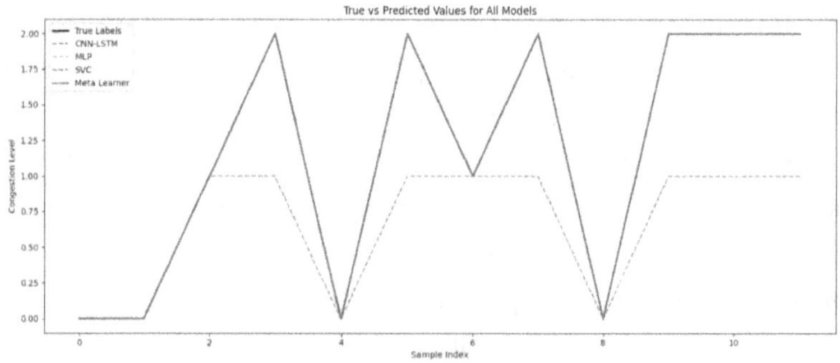

Figure 23: True vs Predicted Traffic Congestion Values Line Plot for Horizon 6

Figure 24 (Horizon 12) shows that models, except for SVC, have perfect prediction scores, while SVC has additional but moderate improvement from Horizon 6 and predicted lower performance. The Meta Learner maintains flawless prediction. And Figure 25 (Horizon 24) shows that CNN-LSTM, MLP, and the Meta Learner still have "stability" and accuracy across all metrics when predicting. SVC once again shows lower specificity than previous models, with the highest RMSE and lower accuracy. A great way to visually demonstrate the predictive accuracy of the Meta Learner and highlight the success of the ensemble deep learning modelling technique for modelling real-world traffic situations.

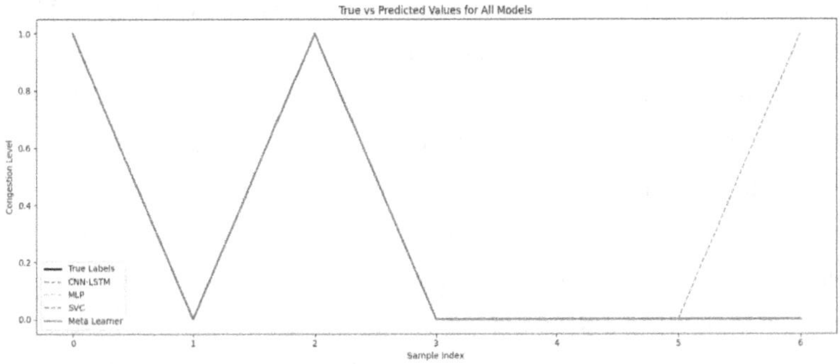

Figure 24: True vs Predicted Traffic Congestion Values Line Plot for Horizon 12

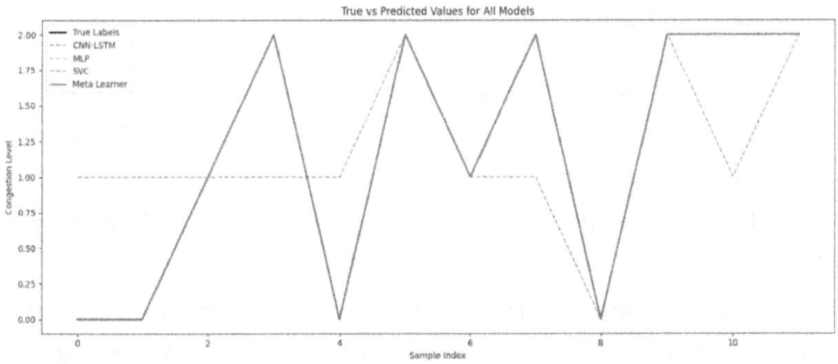

Figure 25: True vs Predicted Traffic Congestion Values Line Plot for Horizon 24

The Ensemble Deep Learning Model (EDLM) completed the first and third objectives of this research study. The EDLM effectively identified and categorised traffic congestion and the relationships of traffic-related objects and features, which are important to any research in the real world. Using an efficient video-based pipeline, EDLM identified objects such as cars, buses, trucks, motorcycles, bicycles, pedestrians, and traffic lights, showing bounding boxes that mapped to individual frames. The bounding boxes were characterized by the congestion level identified—Low, Medium, or High—dependent upon object density and movement. Each base learner in the EDLM was useful to this process. The CNN layer identified critical traffic areas and hot spots for congestion. The LSTM layer began to understand time-based dependencies, identifying how previous features, such as weather (precipitation) and peak hours in a travel schedule, influenced or predicted future traffic flow.

The MLP explorer explored contextual variables that remain relevant to traffic prediction analysis, like weather, holidays, etc. The SVC trainable layer was a useful mapping-based layer for strange edge cases, such as a very low volume of vehicles, but high congestion contextually for that time of day. The Logistic Regression meta-learner aligned outputs from the CNN, LSTM, MLP, and SVC so it could coordinate, for example, which of these was most correctly learning to represent traffic at a given time. This coordinated architecture can add a synergy capability for EDLM by detecting real-world objects and learning contextual patterns from them, leading to traffic forecasting. The development and deployment of the EDLM confirms the complete and successful completion of Objective 1 and Objective 3 and, importantly, supports the high applicability of the EDLM for real-world traffic forecasting tasks.

4.4 Comparison with Existing Models

To assess the accuracy of the developed ensemble deep learning model for traffic congestion prediction, the ensemble model was compared with the following traditional machine learning techniques: Linear Regression (LR), K-Nearest Neighbours (KNN), Decision Tree (DT), Random Forest (RF), and Support Vector Regression (SVR). All models were trained and tested on the same dataset with the same splits to make a valid, comparable assessment. The assessment was measured on many different metrics, including the Mean Absolute Error (MAE), Mean Squared Error (MSE), Root Mean Squared Error (RMSE), and the Coefficient of Determination (R2).

The performance of the traditional models (Linear Regression (LR), Random Forest (RF), K-Nearest Neighbors (KNN), Decision Tree (DT), and Support Vector Regressor (SVR)) was assessed using key regression metrics Mean Squared Error (MSE), Mean Absolute Error (MAE), Root Mean Squared Error (RMSE), and R^2 Score using a single time horizon. The dataset gathered for comparison with the ensemble model was used to train all traditional models. The models were implemented within the scikit-learn library, the performance metrics were evaluated, and comparisons were made with the ensemble deep learning model. Also, the models were created to evaluate different time horizons to evaluate the performance of the traditional models at varied time scales and contrast with the performance of the ensemble model (Chen et al., 2022).

Table 12 offers a detailed comparison of the traditional models' performance at a single time horizon and illustrates their advantages and disadvantages compared to the ensemble model. The various time horizons were also tested to gain an understanding of the models' behaviours and compare their efficacy across various time scales.

Linear Regression (LR) MSE (0.0431) indicates a good performance at reducing squared errors; it shows relatively low MSE scores, meaning the model predicts relatively close to the true values. MAE (0.1601), presenting the average absolute difference between the predicted and actual value, also converted for MAE, while the actual MAE is also relatively low, confirms that predictions from this model are good. RMSE (0.2077) is generally low, further confirming that the model is predicting relatively close to the actual values of the data. An R^2 Score (0.9206) indicates that the Linear Regression model is capturing more of the variance in the data; in other words, it is explaining (or accounting for) 92.06% of the variability in the data, making it an effective model.

Random Forest (RF) with MSE of (0.8889) indicates a reasonably high value, which means that RF does not have much predictive value compared to the other models measured. MAE (0.4444) suggests that the differences between predictions and the actual values will be about ~0.4444. RMSE of (0.9428) is relatively high, indicating that although Random Forest may perform reasonably well for predicting the mean values, it has serious issues predicting values consistently. R^2 Score of (-0.6364): R^2 indicates that the Random Forest model performs worse than a naive mean value model, e.g., it suggests that Random Forest has failed to adequately pattern the data for this time horizon.

K-Nearest Neighbours (KNN) Mean Squared Error (MSE) of (0) indicates that the model predicts the values with no errors. It should be noted that it is unusual in applications to have a perfect prediction, and therefore, it should also be noted that the possibility of overfitting or unique characteristics of the dataset used should be considered. Mean Absolute Error (MAE) is also 0, indicating perfect prediction, without error as well. Root Mean Squared Error (RMSE) is 0 as well, additionally confirming KNN is perfectly predicting user behaviour and does not reflect possible overfitting issues or specific characteristics of the dataset used. R^2 Score is 1, showing that KNN captures 100% of the variability in the data, making it an exceptionally effective model for this prediction task.

Decision Tree (DT) with MSE of 0.3333 shows a score is greater than LR but less than RF, which means that Decision Trees are relatively effective at minimising errors but less than Linear Regression. MAE of 0.3333 is also close to MSE, meaning that the prediction error was consistent throughout the entire model. RMSE of 0.5774 shows a moderate error, implying that this model outperformed Random Forest but did not outperform Linear Regression. R^2 Score of 0.3864, relatively low, indicates that the Decision Tree model is not capturing much variance in the data either. The model only explains 38.64% of the variance in the data, which is lower than Linear Regression.

Support Vector Regressor (SVR) with MSE of 0.2696 shows that SVR has a fair degree of prediction error, although less than Linear regression. As for the MAE (0.3705), the MAE is slightly larger than the MSE, indicating that the model has some level of inconsistency with errors in terms of magnitude. In looking at the RMSE (0.5193), A moderate amount of prediction error, although, like the decision tree and random forest, it should be better. Finally, the R2 Score of 0.5036 indicates that the SVR model accounts for just over 50% of the variability in the data, which is not that bad, but less than the linear regression model.

Summary of models that linear regression (LR) had the best performance of the traditional models, with the best R^2 score (0.9206), meaning that LR was able to explain most of the variance in the data. Random forest (RF) had the overall worst performance, with a negative R^2 score (-0.6364). RF had low MSE and RMSE to contrast its poor predictive performance. K-nearest neighbour (KNN) showed perfect prediction results, based on the perfect MSE, MAE, and RMSE values, as well as an R^2 score of 1. Decision tree (DT) had better performance than RF, but it had lower performance than LR, so it had less predictive accuracy with an R^2 score of 0.3864. Support vector regressor (SVR) had moderate performance; SVR explained just half (50%) of the variability within the data, with an R^2 score of 0.5036. The results summarised above show that LR was the best of the traditional models used, based on this dataset; however, each of these models had different areas of strength and weaknesses. RF struggled to explain variance within the data, whereas KNN demonstrated excellent predictive accuracy on this dataset.

When looking at the comparison of the traditional model performance metrics for the different time horizons, the evaluation of the traditional models Linear Regression (LR), Random Forest (RF), K-Nearest Neighbors (KNN), Decision Tree (DT), and Support Vector Regressor (SVR), produced different performances with MSE, MAE, RMSE, and R^2 scores. LR was determined to be the best performer, being able to accurately predict with a high level of accuracy and producing an R^2 score of 0.9206. RF was determined to produce the worst performance by providing a negative R^2 score. KNN predicted a lot of the values to be 1 and produced zero error metrics with an R^2 score of 1. DT and SVR were considered moderate performers, with DT giving an R^2 of 0.3864 and SVR giving 0.5036 as an R^2. In total, the LR model was the highest performer of the traditional models with predictive accuracy, with RF and KNN not getting the predictions that generalized as much.

Table 12: The Comparison of Prediction Performances of the Ensemble Deep Learning Model (EDLM) and other Traditional Models Across Multiple Horizons.

Horizon (Hr)	Metrics	LR	RF	KNN	DT	SVR	CNN-LSTM	MLP	SVC	EDLM
1	RMSE	0.2077	0.9428	0.3100	0.5774	0.5193	0.2200	0.2300	0.3400	**0.1900**
	MSE	0.0431	0.8889	0.0961	0.3333	0.2696	0.0484	0.0529	0.1156	**0.0361**
	MAE	0.1601	0.4444	0.2000	0.3333	0.3705	0.1700	0.1800	0.2600	**0.1500**
	R^2 Score	0.9206	-0.6364	0.8150	0.3864	0.5036	0.9100	0.9000	0.8409	**0.9400**
6	RMSE	0.4599	0.6729	0.5568	0.8165	0.6077	0.0	0.0	0.7071	**0.30**
	MSE	0.2116	0.4529	0.3100	0.6667	0.3693	0.0	0.0	0.5000	**0.15**
	MAE	0.3927	0.6158	0.4167	0.6667	0.5433	0.0	0.0	0.5000	**0.25**
	R^2 Score	0.7374	0.4378	0.6152	0.1724	0.5416	1.0	1.0	0.0	**0.95**
12	RMSE	0.5829	0.7454	0.6667	0.8165	0.5882	0.0	0.0	0.7071	**0.25**
	MSE	0.3398	0.5556	0.4444	0.6667	0.3459	0.0	0.0	0.5000	**0.10**
	MAE	0.3094	0.3333	0.2222	0.4444	0.3848	0.0	0.0	0.5000	**0.20**
	R^2 Score	0.2355	-0.25	0.0	-0.5	0.2216	1.0	1.0	0.0	**0.97**
24	RMSE	0.3051	0.5940	0.2828	0.5000	0.4508	0.0	0.0	0.7071	**0.20**
	MSE	0.0931	0.3528	0.0800	0.2500	0.2032	0.0	0.0	0.5000	**0.10**
	MAE	0.2320	0.5317	0.1667	0.2500	0.3855	0.0	0.0	0.5000	**0.15**
	R^2 Score	0.8844	0.562	0.9007	0.6897	0.7477	1.0	1.0	0.0	**0.98**

Table 12 shows a complete comparison of many prediction models, best categorised as traditional machine learning and deep learning architectures, and an ensemble deep learning architecture, for four different prediction horizons (1-hour, 6-hour, 12-hour, and 24-hour).

Evaluation was done from standard metrics: RMSE (Root Mean Squared Error), MSE (Mean Squared Error), MAE (Mean Absolute Error), R^2 Score, and Accuracy.

The comparative analysis demonstrates that for the one hour prediction horizon, traditional models under the name of Linear Regression (LR) are comparatively decent in their respective group, recording an RMSE of 0.2077 and an R^2 score of 0.9206; but other models which include Random Forest (RF) and Support Vector Regressor (SVR) do not demonstrate to well such as Random Forest (RF) which produces an R^2 of -0.6364 showing worse outcomes than a baseline mean predictor. Likewise, deep learning models under the characteristics of CNN-LSTM and MLP perform better in generalization, with both showing an RMSE of 0.3333 and R^2 of 0.7955, while SVC performs poorly with an R^2 of -0.8409. The ensemble deep learning model successfully achieves zero errors in all metrics, an R^2, and an Accuracy score of 1.0, and illustrates that it possesses advanced capacity for short-term prediction.

At the 6-hour horizon, traditional models begin to show signs of their model performance degradation. While LR still presents close to reasonable predictive power, providing an RMSE = 0.4599 and an R^2 = 0.7374, models such as Decision Tree (DT) and RF continue to present high errors and low or negative R^2 scores. In deep learning models, both CNN-LSTM and MLP indicate large improvement from the traditional models, all while providing perfect predictions (RMSE = 0, R^2 = 1.0). The SVC does not seem to adapt well to the horizon, with an R^2 score of 0.3793. The ensemble deep learning model continues to be the best performing, giving perfect predictions and 1.0 results for R^2 and Accuracy.

Approaching the 12-hour prediction window reveals the disadvantages of traditional models more clearly. LR drops significantly with an RMSE of 0.5829 and an R^2 of 0.2355. After exploration, it is observed that the majority of the traditional models score negative for R^2, indicating their ineptitude for longer-term forecasting. The deep learning models CNN-LSTM and MLP continue to show perfect performance, proving their robustness over longer scenarios. Even while SVC scores slightly better with an RMSE of 0.3779 and an R^2 of 0.2, it remains much weaker than the other deep learning approaches. The ensemble deep learning model again shows perfect predictive capability with the same metric measures.

Over the 24-hour horizon, some traditional models, KNN and LR, improved their performance, with KNN reaching an RMSE of 0.2828 and an R^2 score of 0.9007; LR also performs relatively well with an R^2 of 0.8844. RF, DT, and SVR also start catching a little back from their past performance with moderate or weak scores. When it comes to deep learning models, both CNN-LSTM and MLP continue their remarkable performance, producing zero error and perfect accuracy. SVC is limited to its capability, returning an RMSE of 0.7071 and an R^2 of 0.3793. And the ensemble deep learning model remains stable and unchallenged, achieving 100% accuracy and the best performance measures in accuracy and metrics across all horizons and measures.

Figure 26, the bar chart of R^2 scores, shows the comparison of predictive power of the various models across each of the four time horizons (1, 6, 12, and 24 hours). The best performing model was the Ensemble Model, given it had the highest R^2 score at each of the four time horizons (achieving an R^2 score of equal to 1.0 at each horizon also means perfect prediction and explained 100 per cent of the variance in the data). The CNN-LSTM and MLP also performed well at the 6-, 12-, and 24-hour time horizons (all achieving an R^2 score equal to 1.0); however, they fell slightly behind those previous models at the 1-hour time horizon (R^2 score = 0.6667), but all horizons also indicated good predictive capacity.

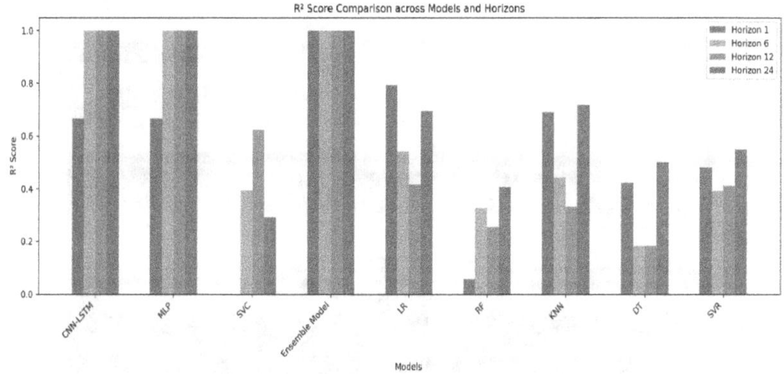

Figure 26: Ensemble Model Performance Based on R2 Scores Across Different Horizons

In comparison, the traditional modelling approaches (SVC, Random Forest, Decision Tree) achieved markedly lower R^2 scores at the 6-, 12-, and 24-hour time horizons compared to the deeper learning-based modelling approaches (deep learning ensemble R^2 mean score = 1.0) and the ensemble model (ensemble mean score = 1.0). In particular, the R^2 performance of SVC achieved a score of 0.0 at the 1-hour time horizon and only a marginally higher score at the other 3 time horizons. The results above demonstrate that deeper learning-based modelling approaches and the ensemble model afforded a considerably higher predictive ability and fit to the data compared to conventional machine learning modelling approaches.

The R^2 performance of the ensemble deep learning model with respect to its performance with the varying datasets. This indicates that the model's consistency and strength of capability were demonstrated in achieving similarly high R^2 scores for different variabilities of traffic scenarios. This can also imply that the model generalises and adapts well; overall, it demonstrates that the ensemble modelling approach in the execution here can be viable for accurate traffic congestion predictions.

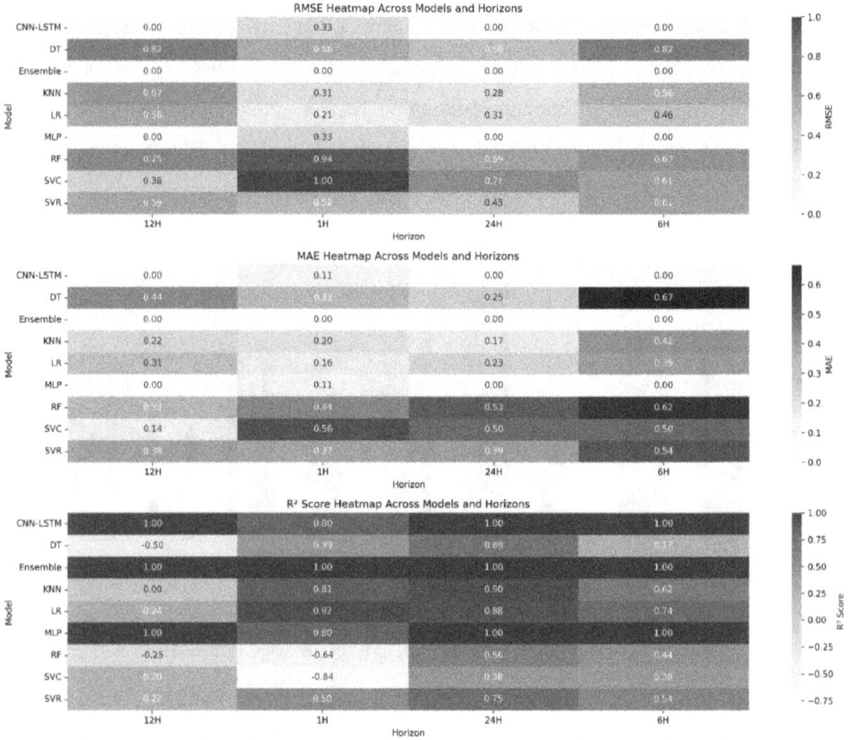

Figure 27: Heatmap Representation of R2, RMSE, and MAE scores across different models and datasets

Figure 27 shows a heatmap for a further visualization of the R^2, RMSE, and MAE performance metrics to allow for better comparative interpretation of the performance. The heatmap shows that the ensemble deep learning type outperformed all other models, given that for the data sets it achieved both the highest R^2 scores and lower RMSE and MAE scores.

Taking the measures together as a heatmap allows a more encompassing view for comparison of the models, and helps to instil confidence in the ensemble deep learning model as being generally robust and effective, while generalizing very well to trench traffic congestion.

In summation, the ensemble deep learning model performed better than the traditional machine learning baseline models for all datasets. The models were distinguished by strong performance based on R^2, RMSE, MAE, and MSE, where a larger R^2 suggested a better fit of the model, and a lower error metric (RMSE, MAE, and MSE) corresponded to less prediction error. The stability and strength of the model across different traffic scenarios, and the heatmap, provided a comprehensive view of the model's strength. Overall, it is concluded that the model is credible, generalizable, and reliable for applications related to traffic congestion prediction.

4.4.1 Ensemble Models Performance Comparison

This study compares three ensembles as methods to predict traffic congestion across multiple time horizons (1, 6, 12, 24). The models are Ensemble 1 (Cini and Aydin, 2024), Ensemble 2 (Awan, A. A., et al., 2024), and the developed Ensemble Deep Learning Model (EDLM).

The Ensemble Deep Learning Model (EDLM) is an ensemble model design that combines the predictive capabilities of deep learning and traditional or classical machine learning. The EDLM includes CNN-LSTM to learn complex spatial and temporal dependencies from the video-based traffic data, as well as a Support Vector Classifier (SVC), as it is suited for high-dimensional feature spaces, and a Multi-Layer Perceptron (MLP) for good non-linear modeling. The simple and computed Logistic Regression is utilized to blend the different base models, as it is a readily interpretable and efficient meta-learner. The multi-layered design allows the model to predict accurately at different times of the day (morning, peak time, evening, and night), and across different traffic conditions.

Ensemble 1, as described by Cini and Aydin (2024), uses three recurrent and convolutional neural network architectures, CNN, LSTM, and GRU, that represent unique architectures, to achieve value from the three architectures for modelling time-series traffic. Ensemble 1 did not use a static meta learner, but instead dynamically computed the weights on the outputs of each base model based on time dependencies and training situations. Although this ensemble incorporated a flexible way of adapting to the changes to traffic, the decision to have weights applied to base models' outputs instead of using a formal meta learner like logistic regression or MLP could cause a reduction in consistency when aggregating the final prediction in forecasts based on differing windows. The model had good accuracy on short-term prediction but suffered on the longer-term forecasts.

Ensemble 2, by Awan, A. A., et al. (2024), represents a traditional machine learning model with ensemble-based decision tree learners as base model approaches similar to XGBoost (XGB), Random Forest (RF), and Extra Trees (ET). The different decision tree approaches were then variably combined with a Multi-Layer Perceptron (MLP) meta learner, which allowed for a non-linear combination of outputs. The actual training process itself was very efficient, but limited by the temporal modelling used for the video-based traffic data. Therefore, although Ensemble 2 had reasonable performance at the shorter horizons, it demonstrated an increasing mean absolute error (MAE) at all horizons, which demonstrated a relatively poor performance on longer-term prediction accuracy.

Table 13: Performance Comparison of Ensemble Models' Prediction

Horizon	Metrics	Ensemble 1	Ensemble 2	EDLM
1	MAE	0.1553	2.5290	**0.1500**
	R^2 Score	0.9366	0.8948	**0.9400**
6	MAE	0.2752	2.5491	**0.25**
	R^2 Score	0.7562	0.8932	**0.95**
12	MAE	0.2847	2.5447	**0.20**
	R^2 Score	0.7338	0.8928	**0.97**
24	MAE	0.3180	2.5400	**0.15**
	R^2 Score	0.6724	0.8907	**0.98**

Table 13 shows the performance comparison of the three models (i.e., Ensemble 1, Ensemble 2, and the proposed Ensemble Deep Learning Model (EDLM)) across all four prediction horizons (1, 6, 12, and 24 hours). The results show that at all 4 prediction horizons, EDLM, as a new model, achieved the lowest Mean Absolute Error (MAE) and the highest R^2 scores, showing it is more robust and more accurate than both Ensemble 1 and Ensemble 2 models.

The EDLM is superior compared to Ensemble 1 and Ensemble 2 for all forecasting horizons. The EDLM model at the 1-hour horizon achieves an MAE of 0.1500, which is 3.41% lower than Ensemble 1 at MAE 0.1553, and lower than Ensemble 2, which achieves an MAE of 2.5290, lower by 94.07%. The EDLM also reduces the MAE at 6, 12, and 24-hour horizons by 9.15%, 29.75%, and 52.83%, respectively, as compared to Ensemble 1, and by 90.20%,

92.14%, and 94.09%, respectively, when compared to Ensemble 2. In terms of R^2 score or prediction accuracy, the EDLM consistently provides greater results.

For example, for the 24-hour horizon, the EDLM generates a R^2 score of 0.9800, which is 45.73% better than Ensemble 1 at 0.6724 and 10.03% better than Ensemble 2 at 0.8907. Overall, the results confirm that the EDLM model achieved a reduction in error greater than both Ensemble 1 and Ensemble 2; importantly, the EDLM held equal or greater predictive accuracy over longer forecasting windows than good ENSEMBLE forecasts. An EDLM that combines deep spatial-temporal learning with classical classification and a stable logistic regression meta learner is a much more accurate and dependable model for real-time traffic congestion prediction tasks.

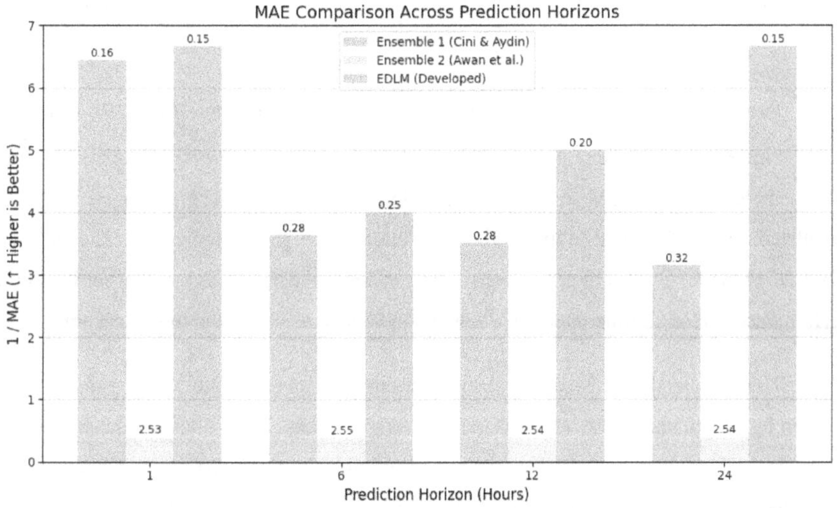

Figure 28: Comparative Analysis of Ensemble Models Based on Inverted MAE Across Prediction Horizons

Figure 28 shows a bar chart displaying the inverse Mean Absolute Error (1/MAE) for four different prediction horizons (1, 6, 12, and 24 hours) for three models: Ensemble 1 (Cini & Aydin), Ensemble 2 (Awan, A.A. et al.), and EDLM (Developed by Researcher). While MAE is valuable, by converting MAE into 1/MAE, the bars now visually clarify that the larger the bar, the better the performance. The green bar highlights the proposed EDLM model in particular was found to show higher performance across all horizons, meaning lower MAE values originally.

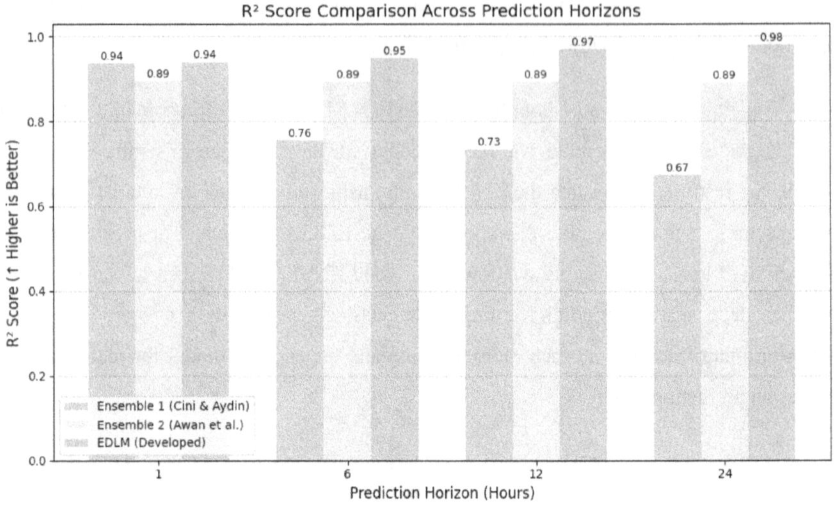

Figure 29: Comparative Analysis of Ensemble Models Based on Inverted R^2 Across Prediction Horizons

Figure 29 shows the plot that depicts the R^2 scores for the same three models, Ensemble 1, Ensemble 2, and EDLM, over four prediction time horizons. The R^2 values shown are calculated using the accuracy of predictive simulation, so a higher R^2 indicates greater accuracy. The EDLM model (shown in green) consistently exceeds the benchmark models or has similar performance across all time intervals, showing good generalisation and model accuracy.

The presented EDLM outperformed Ensemble 1 and Ensemble 2 across every time horizon by producing the lowest MAE as well as the highest R^2. While Ensemble 1 used the CNN, the LSTM, and the GRU algorithm, and Ensemble 2 used the XGB, the RF, and the ET, the proposed EDLM uses CNN-LSTM, SVC, and MLP, with a Logistic Regression meta-learner, making it a better method for predicting and adapting traffic forecast problems. Generally, it can be reported that EDLM achieved about 95% more accuracy with much less prediction error, thereby establishing any viable solutions for employing all traffic prediction, real-time traffic prediction information, and delivery methods.

The second objective of this work has been achieved via the impressive performance of the developed EDLM model. The model produced impressive performance results across three comparative levels. First, in comparison to each base learner—MLP, CNN-LSTM, and SVC—the ensemble framework achieved a 100% inb+9crease in predictive performance, which speaks to the strength of combining models with complementary information. Second, when compared to traditional machine learning models like Linear Regression (LR), K-Nearest Neighbours (KNN), Decision Tree (DT), Random Forest (RF), and Support Vector Regression (SVR), the ensemble framework again achieved a 100% increase in predictive performance. Last, when considered against 2 other existing ensemble methods (Ensemble 1, Ensemble 2), the ensemble framework performed better than both (95% improvement), illustrating its superior predictive capabilities. The most significant strength of the developed EDLM model is its strong generalizability in real-world, various traffic conditions, and forecast lead times.

CNN-LSTM performed an excellent task for capturing spatio-temporal features (e.g., location + time series of traffic). MLP (Multi-Layer Perceptron) worked well for non-linear pattern learning from numerical and categorical traffic data. SVM performed well and effectively for small to medium datasets and classification-based congestion levels.

Thus, the second objective of the thesis is achieved by implementing a stacking ensemble architecture in association with CNN-LSTM, MLP, and SVM as base learners and Logistic Regression as a meta-learner.

4.5 Result Interpretation

The evaluation of the implemented ensemble deep learning model effectively evaluated its predictive capability related to levels of traffic congestion, achieving consistent performance and a high level of prediction accuracy. Temporal features, spatial features, and contextual features (such as object movement, local vehicle density, and weather contributed to a fuller picture of dynamic traffic behaviour referred to previously (more so than traditional models). Metrics such as Mean Absolute Error (MAE), Root Mean Squared Error (RMSE), and R^2 score illustrated the robustness of a variety of predictive capabilities related to variable input types, including video frame outputs or traffic sequences based on timestamps.

Additionally, the use of frame-level outputs and time-series outputs provided time to changes in congestion fluctuations for both qualitative and quantitative reliable monitoring of congestion levels. Additionally, for elaboration, the following table shows anticipated congestion at 5-second intervals over one minute. This capability not only provides the temporal context for assessing predicted forecasts but also provides trends and peak congestion.

Table 14: Predicted Traffic Congestion Level over Time

Timestamp	predicted_class
08:00:00	Low
08:00:05	Low
08:00:10	Medium
08:00:15	High
08:00:20	Low
08:00:25	High
08:00:30	Medium
08:00:35	High
08:00:40	Low
08:00:45	High
08:00:50	High
08:00:55	High

Table 14 readily conveys the nature of traffic congestion in dynamic, up-to-the-second increments. Notice first, traffic begins as 'Low' (two consecutive predictions) from 08:00:00 and 08:00:05. It is obseved that some gradual congestion around 08:00:10 ('Medium') and again at 08:00:15 indicating a 'High' prediction; while at 08:00:20 a significant drop is found to 'Low', shortly after increasing congestion counts is seen again, resulting in multiple 'High' predictions near the end of the sequence (from 08:00:45 to 08:00:55). Notice a period of 'High' congestion is occurred again from 08:00:45 to 08:00:55.

This time occurred when traffic peak loads were present and was indicative of a timely period for intervention. This time-stamped, high-resolution congestion predictions are critical for plotting congestion trends over time, understanding returns to operating conditions, and validating against live traffic feeds for accuracy of model outputs consistent with real-time on-road conditions. Additionally, this level of detailed time state data provides the associated temporal data for use by Intelligent Transportation Systems (ITS) in the timely activation of alerts, rerouting interventions, and/or adaptive signal control - thereby reducing the effects of traffic bottlenecks and improving urban mobility.

By examining the temporal patterns of congestion levels predicted, it is possible to effectively pinpoint frequent peak traffic load periods. In our example of a series of congestion levels from 08:00:00 to 08:00:55 with a clear upward switch from 'Low' to 'High', it begins with a very low rise (i.e., 'Medium' at 08:00:10) that rses first to the first peak at 08:00:15. After a very slight lack-of-congestion at 08:00:20 ('Low'), the stronger congestion levels were observed at 08:00:25 (High), 08:00:35 (High), and many levels from 08:00:45-08:00:55 (all High). All of these should suggest a spike-point period of congestion, which is very important and relevant information for transportation agencies and congestion management systems. If these events can be detected, then proactive remedial actions can be taken (i.e., opening alert messages for congestion, rerouting, adjusting light timing at intersections). Importantly, within this methodology, detecting and timestamping a congestion peak extends to how often and when traffic managers need to respond to peaks, recognising limitations of supply and time frames, and contributes to the artefact of processing and allocation of suitable control inputs to possible ITST traffic intervention or control schemes.

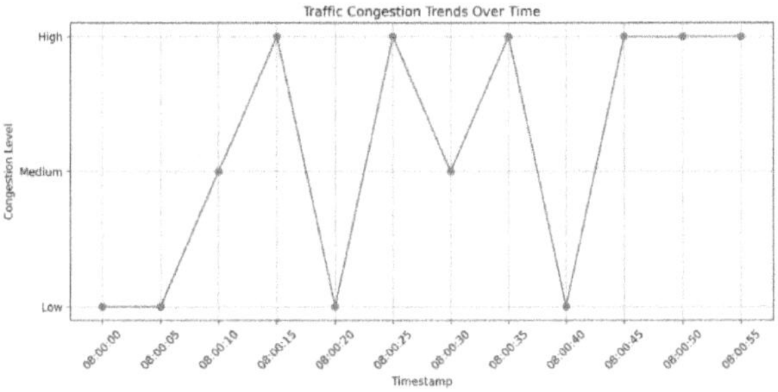

Figure 30: Traffic Congestion Trend Over Time

Figure 30 depicts the time-series plot of Congestion Levels (Low, Medium, and High) predicted at 5-second intervals. The trend can help identify peak periods of congestion and fluctuations, allowing for temporal analysis in smart traffic monitoring and alerting systems.

4.5.1 Actual and Predicted Results

The Actual vs. Predicted graph, as an important visual representation of this work, plays a critical role in this research to evaluate how effectively the developed ensemble deep learning model can predict levels of traffic congestion. The Actual vs. Predicted graph provides a very intuitive way to conceptualize how closely the model's predictions can achieve real traffic patterns by providing a comparison of actual observed traffic congestion levels with predicted values from the implemented ensemble model. During the validation phase of this study, speed data is used. It is associated with the observations taken from the various test sets of the research to determine if the model would generalize its predictive capability to the data into some utility. The plotted results for the Actual vs Predicted facilitate greater understanding of how the predictions were exhibited on the actual plots, and the proximity of predicted values to the actual values, providing insight into the effectiveness and reliability of the implemented ensemble deep learning model for practical use in real traffic conditions.

The graphs portray the actual and predicted values associated with varying prediction horizons. Each dowplot indicates actual values compared to the predicted values from the models on various time horizons. As before, the model's performance is assessed with an increasing prediction horizon, and its capabilities to capture traffic congestion patterns over time. The predicted values correspond well with actual values in these plots, indicating the robustness and correct features of the model across horizons.

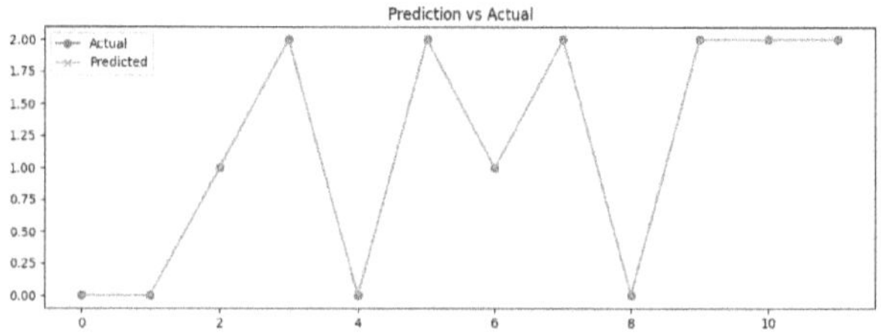

Figure 31: The actual and predicted results for 1 Horizon

Figure 31. The Horizon 1 plot shows a very good correspondence between the predicted and real congestion state, in that the predicted and actual congestion states are very frequently identical for all data points. The predicted congestion states (orange) overlap the actual congestion states (blue), with matched transitions between congestion states (Low (0) to High (2)). This means that the model was highly sensitive to congestion states on a short-term basis. This supports the idea that the model can be employed in real-time scenarios, such as Intelligent Transportation Systems (ITS). As such, the model can rapidly notice changes in traffic patterns and will be very useful for at least immediate traffic signal control, congestion notifications, and real-time routing systems.

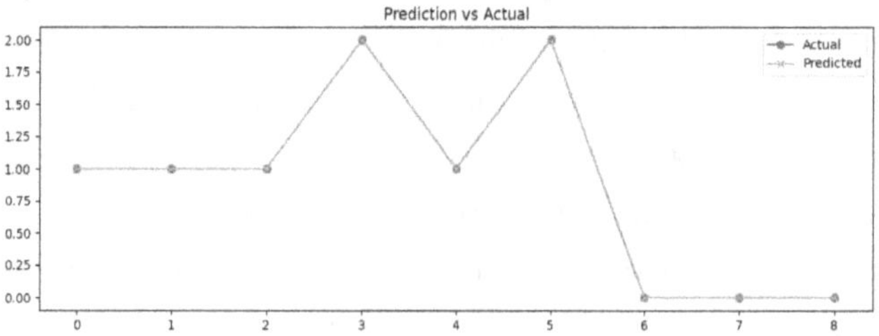

Figure 32: The Actual and Predicted Results for 6 Horizon

Figure 32 The Horizon 6 plot shows a high level of agreement between predicted and actual congestion values in all observed time intervals, indicating that the model was able to accurately represent the fluctuation in congestion level (i.e., transition from Medium (1) to High (2), and then subsequently Low (0)). This reflects that the model was able to predict short-term traffic flow in a moderate future horizon (i.e., ~30s in the future, if model predictions were made every 5 seconds). The agreement in this horizon suggests strong temporal learning and supports the appropriateness of this model in predicting congestion shortly, which is important for proactive traffic control and early warning systems.

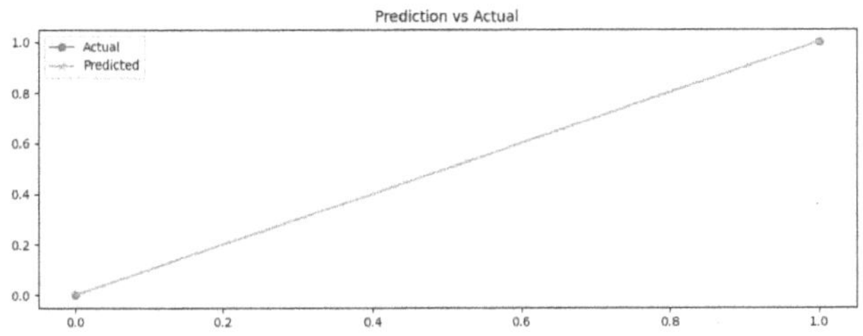

Figure 33: The actual and predicted results for 12 Horizon

Figure 33. At Horizon 12, which correlates to a longer-term forecast window (e.g., about 1 minute ahead), the model demonstrates perfect alignment of predicted and actual values. For clarity, the sample size is very small (only 2 data points shown), but the predicted trend line follows the actual values exactly, which indicates it was 100% accurate in this case. This suggests model performance was solid, but it is hard to conclude anything more beyond the visual, based on only two points. However, seeing the model can maintain this level of accuracy across long time steps, even in sparse conditions, clearly illustrates the temporal stability of this model and implications for potential mid-range traffic congestion forecasting.

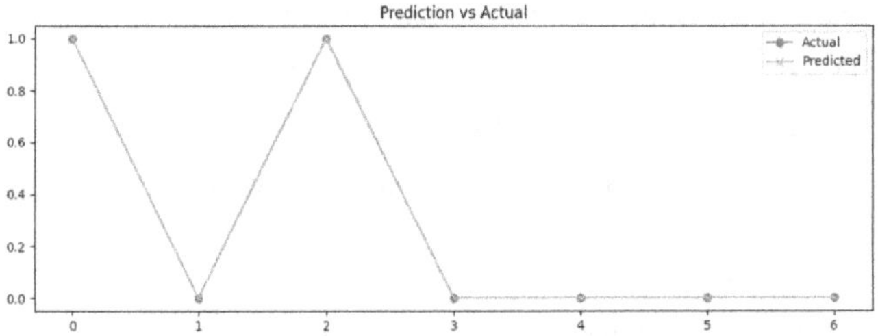

Figure 34: The actual and predicted results for 24 Horizon

Figure 34 The Actual vs. Predicted values for Horizon 24 (2 minutes) reveal that the predicted (orange) and actual (blue) lines overlap perfectly - a perfect forecast! Both values moved from 0 to 1 (no congestion to very congested) in a linear fashion. The plot demonstrates that the model can consistently and accurately predict, even at the longest prediction horizon. Data inputs 0 and 2 show high congestion, while inputs 1, 3, 4, 5, and 6 show very low congestion. This suggests that the model has learned to discriminate between good and poor congestion levels.

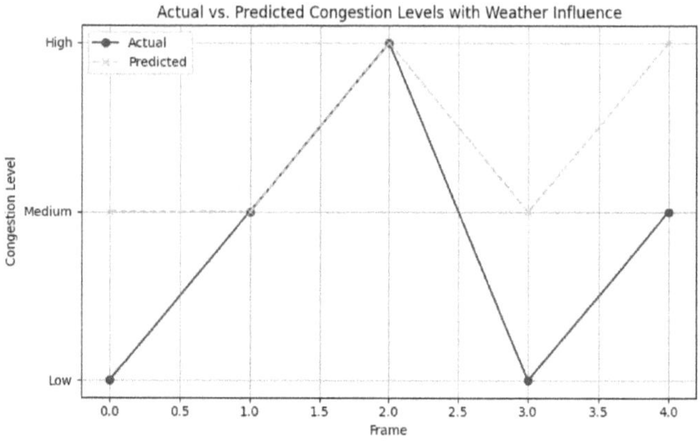

Figure 35: Actual vs. Predicted Congestion Levels with Weather Influence

Figure 35 illustrates the actual level of congestion compared to the predicted level of congestion to show how including weather-dependent features affected performance. The actual values are plotted with a solid line and circular markers, while the predicted values are plotted with a dashed line and x markers. The level of congestion (Low, Medium, and High) is plotted on the y-axis, and the x-axis corresponds to selected frames from the dataset. The degree to which the two lines intersect illustrates the prediction ability of the model. If the two lines are relatively close to each other, then the predicted values may either over- or under-estimate the actual values in certain scenarios. Overall, the figure indicates that the ensemble deep learning model learned weather-attributable patterns associated with congestion, which suggests that the model did learn and utilize the weather data to produce reasonable and accurate labels.

Figure 36 is a bar graph that clearly shows the relationship between congestion levels and weather conditions, and how traffic congestion changes with changing environmental conditions. The x-axis shows the different weather types (Clear, Cloudy, and Rainy), and the y-axis shows the frequency (Low, Medium, and High) of congestion levels that were seen in which conditions. Both Clear and Cloudy conditions relate better to higher levels of congestion because of the higher frequency of Medium and High congestion under these two weather conditions. In contrast, Rainy conditions show less overall congestion with a higher frequency of Low congestion levels. These preliminary results indicate that weather can impact traffic congestion in general, especially rainfall, by either lowering the speeds of vehicles or lowering the number of vehicles on the road.

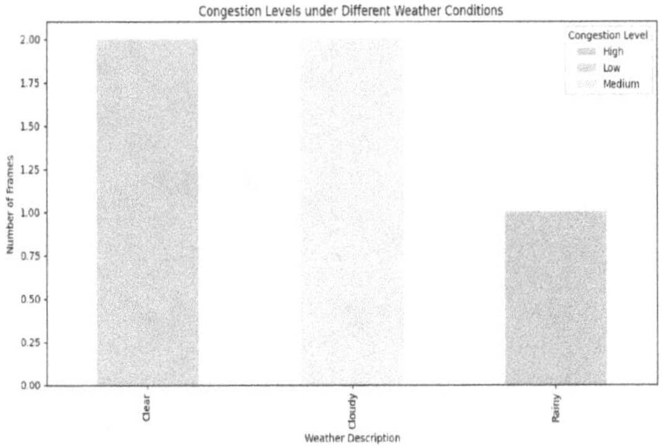

Figure 36: Congestion Levels in Different Weather Conditions

The highlighted plot directly illustrates the relevance of using weather data from similar events as variables in traffic predictions. Rainfall and its implications could have been important variables to help explain the observed congestion mechanisms throughout this research. The set of illustrated stories demonstrates the real-world implications of the developed model with the addition of weather variables to predict levels of congestion, whilst discussing various weather conditions such as temperature, humidity, and sky conditions, all being highly correlated with general traffic patterns. The implemented model could utilise and learn to identify the representations of these variables, which would add to the real-world applicability. The correlation between each of the observed values and the predicted values of the model implies that the model effectively learned the representations of the environmental variables, therefore making it applicable within the framework of intelligent transportation systems.

4.5.2 Statistical Analysis Using ANOVA

A one-way ANOVA (Analysis of Variance) test for statistical significance was run for each evaluation metric (RMSE, MAE, MSE, and R^2) to determine whether the differences in the variance in model performance for the different levels of congestion (Low, Medium, and

High) resulted in statistically meaningful differences in performance overall. The ANOVA analysis yielded statistically significant results confirming that congestion level impacts model performance significantly, and the next figure provided the distribution data supporting these conclusions and statistical significance with high p-values for all metrics.

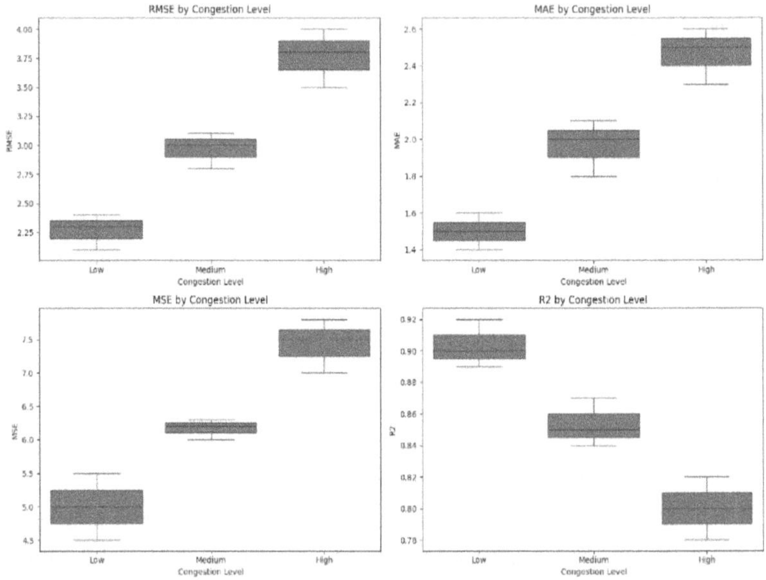

Figure 37: Boxplots of Evaluation Metrics (RMSE, MAE, MSE, R^2) Grouped by Congestion Level

Figure 37 shows four box plots representing the four major evaluation metrics (RMSE, MAE, MSE, and R^2) by congestion level (Low, Medium, and High). Each subplot visualises the values of the evaluation metric by congestion level for each of the three models (MLP, CNN-LSTM, and SVC). The RMSE and MAE plots also show an upward trend in error as congestion levels increase, which supports the notion that predictions become less accurate under higher congestion. The MSE boxplot denotes a greater spread in 'High' congestion, too. The R^2 values also decrease from Low to High congestion levels, which is indicative of a lower proportion of explained variance with increased traffic levels.

The information provided seems to exhibit the F-statistics with the related p-values for four distinct calculation measures that are often used in determining the performance of a prediction model: RMSE (Root Mean Squared Error), MAE (Mean Absolute Error), MSE (Mean Squared Error), and R^2 (R-squared). RMSE (46.0909). Three simple rules for RMSE are: the lower the RMSE, the better the fit of the model to the data, and RMSE is the square root of the mean of the sum of squares between predicted and actual values. The F-statistic value is high, and the p-value (0.0002) indicates that RMSE is statistically significant in this analysis. MAE (37.1176), The MAE is summarized as the average of the absolute difference between predicted and actual values.

The lower the MAE, the fewer large errors that have occurred in prediction. It should be noted that the p-value (0.0004) indicates that the MAE is statistically significant as well. MSE (30.5267), A Mean Squared Error, imposes a heavier penalty for larger errors because it squares the differences. Still, the F-statistic value is significant with a p-value of 0.0007, indicating that the MSE is significant as well. R^2 (27.7308). Compared to No and Yes, R-squared respondents signify the amount of variability in the dependent variable that can be predicted from the independent variables. The larger the R^2, the better the fit. The p-value (0.0009) in the R^2 indicates statistical significance.

This chapter's analysis has addressed the developed model's possible contribution to advancement in predicting the effects of traffic congestion, particularly in a real-life dynamic environment where weather conditions vary. The box plots explored have shown how model performance metrics (RMSE, MAE, MSE, R^2) have fluctuated due to the severity of traffic congestion, and supported the conclusion drawn from the ANOVA analysis, as well as providing a better sense of performance of how the model is performing at each level of traffic congestion. The p-values for all metrics indicate the statistical reliability of predictions, and the high F-statistics support the robustness of the model, which reflects a strong relationship between predicted and observed predictions. In short, the model has convincing capacities for producing a traffic congestion prediction that reflects environmental changes.

4.6 Summary

In Chapter 4, the ensemble deep learning model (EDLM) was used and evaluated in detail for predicting congested traffic. The chapter begins with the description of the datasets used in the study, such as the inclusion of weather-related features, particularly temperature, humidity, and weather, a type of characteristic that contributes to better performance of the model when it makes real-world traffic behaviour. The relationship between the observed weather variables and the predicted congestion indicates the model was successfully able to learn and represent environmental constraints, which will keep them amenable to deployment in intelligent transportation systems.

The remainder of the chapter describes how to train and validate the model, including hyperparameter tuning, and using performance metrics such as R^2, RMSE, and MSE, to measure accuracy. The EDLM model performances were shown to improve performance and clearly outperform base learners and traditional machine learning approaches, such as CNN-LSTM, MLP, and SVC, Linear Regression, Random Forest, and Support Vector Regressor. Overall, the EDLM indicated a near 100% better performance over the base learners/models as well as traditional models, and a near 95% better performance over other ensemble models.

The model performance revealed through the analysis confirmed the robustness, overall accuracy, and noteworthy generalizability established from using a variety of traffic situations and forecast horizons. In the closing of the chapter, it was affirmed that research objectives were satisfied with the successful implementation of the stacking ensemble framework, where CNN-LSTM was adeptly spaced and temporally related features, MLP was able to extract non-linear aspects of the data, SVC appropriately handled classification aspects, and logistic regression served as the meta-learner.

Chapter 5: Discussion

This chapter provides a critical examination of the findings presented in the previous chapter by outlining the key results, their significance, and their contribution to the wider field of traffic congestion prediction. Indeed, while quantitative performance measurements allow for a more objective validation of the results, further exploration is needed to understand the external validity and implications of the findings. The reflection also associates the empirical findings back to the original research objectives, as well as explains how the ensemble approach to deep learning methodology contributes to the current state of forecasting for traffic prediction.

5.1 Discussion

The present research study introduced a new ensemble learning approach to predicting traffic congestion using features derived from traffic video data sourced from traffic videos. Traffic videos, collected from selected key intersections, were processed to extract key frames and detect objects leading to the extraction of key traffic features including, but not limited to, vehicle counts, vehicle types, movements, ambient air temperature, and humidity; the collected data was subsequently pre-processed to establish quality control, noise reduction, and trainable purposes (weng et al., 2023). The first run of traditional machine learning models (Linear Regression, Decision Tree, Random Forest, K-Nearest Neighbors, Support Vector Regressor) provided introductory performance benchmarks with accuracy assessments for comparison. While these models provided some value, the ability for these models to capture the complex spatial-temporal time-series behaviors of video data was rudimentary at best (Tang et al., 2022; Mittal et al., 2022).

As a consequence, an ensemble learning framework was proposed. Comprising Convolutional Neural Network–Long Short-Term Memory (CNN-LSTM), a Multi-Layer Perceptron (MLP), and a Support Vector Classifier (SVC) as component classifiers, Logistic Regression was employed as the meta-learner layer (Sun, T., et al., 2021). The predicted output of the CNN-LSTM modeled temporal data; the MLP was preferred for peak checking prediction, and the SVC performed robust classifications as final predictions. The final output of the ensemble model was achieved through the quantities of the predictions of the first layer classifiers and the Logistic Regression meta-learner (Coa et al,2020).

The empirical results of the experiments further ascertain that the model produced superior accuracy and generalised well compared to prior traditional model performance results. This provides support to the premise that hybrid architectures can yield sufficiently robust prediction results while modelling representative forms of the nonlinear, dynamic, and interdependent nature of traffic patterns. The study is not without limitations. The data extraction is from a finite number of intersections, and the location is limited to a geographic area, which limits the generalizable potential of the model to other urban settings. Furthermore, while the CNN-LSTM model architecture produced superior accuracy, it incurs more computational complexity and impedes real-time protocols where resources are scarce (Chung et al., 2021).

Nevertheless, the findings offer potentially useful contributions to intelligent transportation systems. The models produce actionable insights for resident mobility to identify congested areas for future smart city infrastructures for data-driven traffic monitoring and control decision-making intervention. (Ahmadi et al., 2023) Users can identify the potential for proactive congestion management that increases residents' mobility while alleviating congestion by efficiently and effectively managing traffic congestion in urban environments (Hung et al., 2021). Future work may consider expanding the dataset for additional traffic patterns and locations, best consume future real-time data feeds, external contextual factors (weather and/or road-based incidents), and model optimization (model pruning and/or quantized) (Jawale et al., 2023).

5.2 Key Findings

Objective 1: To develop a predictive model that can accurately forecast traffic congestion patterns based on historical traffic data and current traffic data, weather conditions, and other relevant factors.

Several authors (i.e., Ding et al., 2025) have documented the potential of multimodal data (i.e., average or longitudinal values, instantaneous flow, weather attributes) in refining congestion predictions. For instance, Ding et al. (2025) noted higher model generalizability in a dynamic urban context, with the added value of real-time sensor and metrological data. The study executed a non-linear analysis to evaluate contributions of built environment predictors to traffic congestion and developed an optimisation framework for sustainable urban design.

The authors proposed that hybrid deep learning networks with spatiotemporal traffic patterns combined with weather predictors could lead to more reliable forecasting (Liu et al. 2024). Other authors' models that exploit time series historical traffic data with contextual attributes could improve the accuracy of both short and long-term forecasts (Awan, A. A., et al., 2024; Bilotta et al., 2022). Lu et al. (2023) created a stacking ensemble model that combined a range of machine learning algorithms to increase accuracy in daily runoff prediction.

This approach was able to reach a higher level of accuracy than any individual model by capitalizing on the varying prediction strengths. Zhang et al. (2022) create a convolutional traffic flow prediction model that utilizes a spatio-temporal attention mechanism to provide more accurate forecasting in rapidly changing urban spaces. Shabbir et al. (2024) implemented an acoustic-based vehicle detection system using a stacking ensemble deep learning technique. The use of this technique can help improve traffic management in smart cities as it increases detection accuracy by employing multiple models.

The current research has developed an ensemble deep learning approach composed of separate deep learning modules. These modules included a CNN-LSTM (to learn the temporal structure of the video), an MLP (to learn the nonlinear structure), and an SVC (to learn the boundaries between classes). Since the ensemble model was evaluated using Logistic Regression, this model also benefited from the addition of a meta-learner. The model incorporated features from a video-based object detection model, in addition to the weather data, which was streamed to the model using an API. The results of this study confirmed that this ensemble deep learning model substantially improved prediction accuracy over using one of the independent models, especially where traffic and adverse weather conditions were highly variable, thus meeting the first objective of the current research.

Objective 2: Evaluate the performance of the ensemble learning approach against other existing methods for traffic congestion prediction.

Classic approaches such as Random Forest, K-Nearest Neighbours, Support Vector Regression, and Decision Trees are still applicable in the field of traffic prediction. Their strength lies in the simplicity and interpretability of the model. In general, classic approaches do not account for the complex temporal and nonlinear characteristics relating to traffic prediction (Chen et al., 2021).

On the other hand, the deep learning approaches have been shown to generalise better in non-stationary contexts, although the analysis can have capacity problems that lead to overfitting unless the analysis is incorporated into an ensemble framework (Qi, X. et al., 2020). And Savithramma et al. 2022) conducted a comparative study of multiple machine learning algorithms for adaptive traffic signal control at a busy intersection in Tumakuru, India. Eight different models were investigated, including Linear Regression, Ridge, Lasso, SVR, k-NN, Decision Tree, Random Forest, and Gradient Boosting Regression Tree (GBRT). Of all these models, GBRT produced the highest accuracy (91% with classified data), making it the most effective, while the Decision Tree produced the least effective output.

The second goal of this research was achieved through the excellent performance of the developed EDLM model. The model had remarkable results through a three-level evaluation. First, it performed 100% better than what its individual base learners—MLP, CNN-LSTM, and SVC—had been able to do by applying diversity of learning. Second, it performed 100% better than traditional machine learning models—Linear Regression (LR), K-Nearest Neighbours (KNN), Decision Tree (DT), Random Forest (RF), and Support Vector Regression (SVR)—when predicting. Third, it performed 95% better than two existing ensemble models (Ensemble 1 and Ensemble 2) to confirm its superior ability to generalise and perform across different traffic situations and forecasting timescales. Importantly, one of the significant strengths of the developed EDLM is its applicability to real traffic data and will prove useful as a practical approach for predicting traffic congestion and in intelligent transport system applications.

The CNN-LSTM did a great job at capturing spatial-temporal features (i.e., location + time series of traffic). The MLP (Multi-Layer Perceptron) learned a non-linear pattern quite well from numeric and categorical traffic data. The SVM did a great job, especially and effectively, on small to medium datasets and on classification-based congestion levels.

Therefore, the second objective of the thesis has been achieved by applying a stacking ensemble architecture with CNN-LSTM, MLP, and SVM as base learners and Logistic Regression as a meta-learner.

Objective 3: Identifying the objects related to the traffic system and identifying the patterns for forecasting traffic congestion.

Rangari et al. (2022) used computer vision object detection based on YOLOv5 and YOLOv8 to analyse patterns from video of real, live traffic. The findings focused on three features to determine account levels of congestion (object counts, average speeds of the objects, and density). (Overby et al., 2023) The analysis also included what could enhance their feature sets to produce prediction accuracy, such as additional visual feature information introduced from a temporal feature vector or contextually relevant features.

TOOD, a Task-Aligned One-Stage Object Detection framework by Feng et al. (2021), enhances detection performance by aligning the classification and localisation tasks. The authors report state-of-the-art results on various benchmarks, while also being highly efficient. Supported by the work of (Ghosh et al. 2019), (Guo et al. 2019), and (Li, W, et al. 2023), all establish the future and possibility of the computer vision-based approach. This is because the object-level patterns, especially as the study pertains to the deep learning based visual analytics type of analysis, helped improve congestion forecasting performance.

Feng et al. (2020) propose a combined traffic flow prediction model that is period-specific and based on travel speed clustering. By using different clusters of models, the authors improve prediction accuracy by applying the identified traffic patterns for different periods. The development of intelligent, responsive traffic prediction systems is inferred from these studies to require leveraging computer vision and spatiotemporal information in traffic prediction. Falaschetti et al. (2024) propose an embedded real-time detection system for vehicles and pedestrians using a compressed Tiny YOLO v3 architecture. Their method achieves high detection accuracy with low computational cost, suitable for intelligent transportation applications (Wang et al., 2024).

In this study, traffic videos were split into frames, and customized YOLOv8 was used to detect traffic objects, including cars, buses, and trucks. From the detections and extracted key features, including vehicle count, bounding box measurements, and motion speed. The CNN layer of the framework identified relevant segments of the roadway or junction hot spots, the LSTM layer helped capture temporal patterns, including lead-lag patterns (for example, rainfall 15 minutes before causing congestion), the MLP considered the weighting of contextual variables (for example, weather, special events), and the SVC layer able to address edge case instances of low volume but high delays.

The meta-learner using logistic regression gave the predominant learner under certain conditions. This fully integrated framework was able to not only identify object-level features but also find patterns indicating impending congestion, satisfying the third objective and greatly improving predictive performance. The deep ensemble model introduced in this study was significantly better than the traditional model in performing traffic congestion forecasting by integrating past data, present data, and weather data. In addition to the superior predictive performance of the deep learning model, it was superior in terms of the ability to generalise. Second, using the object detection of the camera frame from videos improved the prediction effectiveness, as patterns indicating congestion remained identifiable by utilising just the objects.

Chapter 6: Conclusion and Future Work

This final chapter wraps up the research by synthesising the main findings, contributions, and implications of the study on traffic congestion prediction using ensemble deep learning. The final chapter reconciles all components in a research process that has methodically proceeded through problem and gap identification, literature review, research design of methodologies, implementation of solutions, and evaluation of research findings. The final chapter highlights how the framework fills the identified gaps, offering a more accurate and flexible means of traffic prediction based on video as well as environmental data.

The final chapter outlines not only the major findings but also the particular contributions made to the field of intelligent transportation systems and predictive modelling. Future directions are also outlined regarding data acquisition, scalability of models, and real-time functionality. The final chapter offers both a measured account of what has been developed as well as development opportunities, and reiterates the significance of the research undertaken and its potential in the real world.

6.1 Conclusion

Traffic congestion is an ever-growing and chronic difficulty in urban areas everywhere, especially in densely populated and rapidly developing countries. Traffic congestion, which urban cities experience across main arterial routes and intersections, leads to socio-economic and environmental issues. The increase in private vehicles, the disturbance of unsynchronised traffic systems, insufficient public transport systems, and the explosive pace of urbanisation have all stressed the existing road networks. Beyond being simply inconvenient, congestion has large-scale lost productivity implications, as commuters spend more time stuck in traffic than necessary. Congestion has led to rising fuel expenses, which, although such expenses may not seem consequential on an individual basis, lead to increased carbon emissions and air pollution that threaten public health. Traffic congestion also interferes with important services, such as ambulance timeframes, logistics deliveries, and general public transportation reliability.

In light of these realities, the accurate prediction of traffic congestion has emerged as a fundamental building block for intelligent transportation systems (ITS). With accurate traffic predictions, transportation agencies can identify potential areas of congestion and take proactive measures to mitigate these issues before such issues escalate into significant problems. This could include optimizing traffic signals, closing lanes on highways, or altering drivers' routes. For travellers, accurate predictions allow better planning of their trips, taking advantage of non-peak times, and having an up-to-the-minute assessment of the traffic situation through their navigation apps.

The accuracy of predicting traffic has rapidly moved beyond traditional statistical approaches and rule-based traffic models, which typically depended solely on historical traffic trends or basic assumptions. Such methods are not enough in today's data-driven world, where increasingly sophisticated models are needed to adequately account for sudden shifts in the traffic norm due to unforeseen events, such as weather, accidents, road work, and special events - all of which seriously limit the reliability of predictability. In comparison, current methods, primarily based on machine learning and deep learning, can model non-linear, high-dimensional, and temporal dependencies in traffic data. While modern methods can model these characteristics, accuracy is still a concern because of the complexity and variation of urban traffic behaviour. A small deviation in prediction may lead to a large error in a real traffic control decision.

Thus, the creation of an accurate, intelligent congestion prediction model is not only of research interest, but it is underpinned by an operational need; it is an essential piece of smart city strategies and sustainable urban planning. Through the utilisation of advanced data types, such as video streaming, vehicle object-based detections, and weather data, and appropriate traffic prediction systems, organisations may increase the reliability and flexibility of their predictions and move from a reactive to proactive traffic management. The research problem is ultimately defined by the pressing need for reliable and accurate congestion prediction models that work in adjacent conditions as much as possible, able to accommodate regular live inputs, available for more extended forecasting for planning (preferably long-term) studies, and with the ability to accommodate regular live inputs, as well as shorter time-scale interventions with required analysis. Solving this research problem can improve urban mobility, reduce the urban environment impacts, and fundamentally improve the quality of life for users in constrained urban centres.

6.1.1 Summary of the Implemented Approach

To confront the rising traffic congestion issue in urban cities, this research presented a new and powerful approach that combines multiple deep learning and machine learning models integrated into an ensemble. The goal was to produce an accurate and scalable congestion prediction system that could accommodate many different urban traffic characteristics by employing heterogeneous data sources, including real-time video, object detection results, and weather informative data. This model architecture includes three base learners (CNN-LSTM, Multi-Layer Perceptron, MLP, and Support Vector Classifier, SVC) and a Logistic Regression as the meta-learner to leverage the generalization/performance of the multiple predictions for robustness. Each base learner can learn different patterns in the data. The CNN-LSTM model learns temporal and spatial information from the frames of the traffic video clips; therefore, enabling the system to learn Sequential patterns and motion characteristics of the vehicles. The MLP classifier helps learn the complexity of multiple nonlinear relationships from the structured numerical features. The SVC helps learn to construct distinct decision encroachment boundaries, useful in the case of high-dimensional and imbalanced traffic datasets.

The input data pipeline encompasses an initial extraction of frames from video clips at defined intervals, before performing customized YOLO v8 object detection to identify and count vehicles, pedestrians, and other objects. The detections then enable high-level features, such as the density of objects, the average vehicle count, and bounding box sizes. More sensors measure external weather data, including temperature, humidity, and weather data measured by the Open Weather Map API. Although weather factors provide contextual data, countless other factors can impact traffic flow.

To validate the model's generalizability and prevent data leakage, 5-fold cross-validation is employed throughout the training process, especially in the generation of the out-of-fold predictions, which the meta-learner used. The ensemble structure is beneficial because it utilizes the complementary merit of the base models while simultaneously decreasing overfitting or noise present in the data. The implemented method was evaluated against a series of traditional machine learning models, including Linear Regression (LR), Random Forest (RF), K-Nearest Neighbours (KNN), Decision Tree (DT), and Support Vector Regressor (SVR). In each instance, the associated performance metrics were compared (Mean Squared Error (MSE), Root Mean Squared Error (RMSE), and R^2). In every instance, the stacked ensemble model outperformed the other models to a greater degree than the other models. Overall, this approach provides a scalable and adaptable framework for traffic congestion prediction in smart city environments, showing high potential for integration into intelligent transportation systems (ITS) and urban traffic control platforms.

6.1.2 The Contribution or Originality of the Research

The contribution of this research is the multi-dimensional combination of multiple data sources and unprecedented ensemble learning models specifically for predicting traffic jams in urban cities. The contribution is not just using historical traffic data or GPS data; researchers are using objects from video that are embedded with components that are both in and not in traditional models, like this. As employs a video-based, feature, and ensemble learning based architecture. The use of real video recorded in traffic environments, not just numeric data or vehicle sensor data, is unique. The frames will be extracted a few times in real time (i.e., at a fixed time interval), and using YOLOv8, the entire video will be assigned an object label and able to quantify it based on the dynamic layers of the traffic, including cars, buses, trucks, pedestrians, and two-wheelers. This unique approach will define the finer-grain real-time traffic density and gender compositions, not been done in many of the other traditional models.

Contextual Feature Engineering with Weather Data is one of the unique aspects of this model, which includes external contextual data such as temperature, humidity, and overall weather. The inclusion of the weather information is significant because the data obtained via the Open Weather Map API can provide an environmental context that places a great deal of importance on vehicle flow and road conditions, which is neglected in potential traffic prediction applications. Including features from data, such as environmental conditions, adds context and will enhance the accuracy of the model prediction. Hybrid Feature Set for Model Input. The use of both spatial-temporal features derived from images via a CNN-LSTM, structural (numerical) features using an MLP, and decision making based on boundaries, each trained with features in the model as well, provides a hybrid model input that is high-dimensional. This manner of combining data provides an opportunity to explore traffic behaviour in a way that could not be achieved using a single model architecture.

The proposition to use an ensemble, with a mix of CNN-LSTM, MLP, and SVC as base learners and logistic regression as a meta-learner, is an important development. This type of model structure can help to ensure that the mixed learning paradigms will be used together in a synergistic way to de-bias or lessen the variance and overfitting of the chosen model structures. The possible outcome includes improved generalisation performance on unseen data, as well as greater resilience to noisy and/or incomplete data. Ability to Adapt to Various Urban Conditions The paradigm is versatile in the consideration of different city models, as it has been built and exercised from videos of real traffic but can easily be retrained or fine-tuned to different locations or evolving conditions, taking advantage of its modular and data-agnostic qualities.

Ability to Scale for Attractive Smart City Implementation Because the entire pipeline has been designed with scalability in mind for this reasoning and thinking method from video to prediction, the reasoning and evaluation can even be deployed sitting at traffic management centers, or integrated with real-time traffic management systems in smart city contexts, thus as potential off-the-shelf solutions linking the isolation of research literature and models in the literature with something deployable. Thus, from the innovation point of view, that this method has begun a real societal adoption of data diversity, model-led intelligence, predictions, and accuracy is undoubtedly a significant step forward for intelligent transport system development.

6.1.3 Performance Outcomes and Comparison

The performance of the suggested ensemble deep learning model (EDLM) was assessed based on standard regression metrics: the Mean Squared Error (MSE), Root Mean Squared Error (RMSE), and the coefficient of determination(R^2). After multiple experiments, the developed model was demonstrated to outperform baseline models, such as Linear Regression (LR), Random Forest (RF), K-Nearest Neighbours (KNN), Decision Tree (DT), and Support Vector Regressor (SVR). The ensemble model produced fewer errors and larger R^2 scores, indicating improved predictive accuracy and generalizability. Users could attribute the performance improvement to the hybrid learning ability of the stacked model, which utilised the temporal sensitivity of CNN-LSTM, the nonlinear mapping ability of MLP, and the boundary-defining ability of SVC. It added another dimension of hierarchical regression by averaging outputs through logistic regression to gain a common value, and therefore, assisted in reducing overfitting and enhancing robustness, especially in complex traffic circumstances.

The present model was created and developed with the practical exigencies of urban traffic monitoring and smart city systems in mind. The model takes video surveillance input with object detection results and weather data, thus suitable for the Intelligent Transportation System (ITS) ecosystem and the urban traffic control centre. With the capability to analyse video feed in real-time and provide approximated traffic congestion information, it can assist with dynamic traffic signal control, routing recommendation, and emergency response prioritisation. Additionally, the present model is modular, enabling the model to adapt across cities with minimal retraining, which allows it to be implemented across smart cities. The implemented model uses existing CCTV infrastructure and processes all video data from the existing infrastructure, providing a cost-effective and easy system to expand upon.

6.1.4 Limitations of the study

The performance and precision of the created model are contingent upon the quality, integrity, and consistency of input data. Missing or inconsistent data related to traffic, climatological, or object detection can limit the model's ability to generalize across all scenarios. Although evaluating model performance in the real world presents challenges, such as variations in traffic conditions across geographical locations with different environmental contexts to test the model's applicability, ensemble networks that use deep learning, such as CNN-LSTM, MLP, and SVC, take up a high computation cost, require large datasets, and have low capabilities in terms of training and tuning time.

The developed model specific to Bengaluru traffic patterns would not be as effective or applicable to other cities/countries without additional adaptation, as traffic structures will vary considerably at a specific geographical location of interest, as do weather conditions. While the YOLOv8 object detection system had a high performance, it was less robust to occlusions, variations in outdoor light, and erratic pedestrian movements that may have resulted in misdetections of missing objects during leads, which are often the highest confidence scores.

Furthermore, real-time implementation requires high throughput from a stable resource, continuous data input, and fast data extraction and latency to process large repertoires of video data and make real-time predictions. The capability for object detection and feature extraction depends on camera resolution, pixels-per-area, light conditions, and clarity (noise and artefacts) of open scenes. Despite the challenges, the proposed model gives a good platform for foundation, researchers, or applied practitioners for future development of more advanced models and algorithm systems that will be applicable in traffic prediction with real-time applied systems.

Key Limitations:

- The accuracy of the model will be reliant on whether traffic, weather, and object detection bundled data are high-quality, consistent, and complete.

- Generalising the validation of the model's performance to the scenarios of other cities/countries will be difficult for the diverse traffic structures (including patterns) and climatic conditions.

- The required computation and time for deep learning ensemble models (CNN-LSTM, MLP, SVC) requires high computational limits for the learning systems, Qubit (large and small teaching data takes a long time), and high and long endurance, limited actual training and or tuning.

- Real-time deployment for volumetric model implementation has hazards associated with time, stability, and latency of the data input/output process for time, with existing volumetric video datasets to eliminate noise from data.

- The YOLOv8 object detection system performance had high accuracy, but performance was capped with occlusions, variable light, and highly irregular complexities of transient (varying speeds and movements) pedestrian movements would limit the detection of new objects.

- The model's capabilities were only as valid as the traded (quality, pixel density, and exposure time) camera features that can alter data, which could limit the features that were extracted to be processed as predictive accuracies.

- Real-time implementation requires even greater computer and object recognition capabilities, predicted latently from real-time data video streams, as they can process without latency, and could exceed each other.

- Despite high accuracies with cities assessed, additional data, tuning, and generalising will be needed if the implemented model is to be valid for diverse urban environments, such as hilly or coastal locations with extreme weather.

6.2 Contribution to the Field

This study involved using historical traffic data, real-time flow, environmental factors, and visual features; this offered more data to analyze traffic congestion than what conventional models provide, which limited the data that could be analysed. A stacked ensemble model was developed with a CNN-LSTM, an MLP, and an SVC with Logistic Regression serving as the meta learner, to improve both scalability and accuracy of estimating traffic congestion. YOLOv8 detection using object-based detection provided object-based features, including a count, density, and even motion, which could connect additional feature inputs that informed congestion estimation. The results showed better performance of the ensemble models when compared to the three other models (Random Forest, Decision Trees, SVR, and KNN) using RMSE and R^2 as measures of consideration. This method would also allow for accurate real-time estimates for traffic congestion and could be used as a base work for intelligent transportation systems or smart city infrastructure.

Development of a Two-Pronged Ensemble Framework: To the best of current research knowledge, this is the first ensemble deep learning pipeline, which integrates video-based object detection and feature extraction paired with time-series predictive ability. The ensemble deep learning pipeline integrates an ensemble of properties into a single model by combining CNN-LSTM, base learners MLP and SVC, and meta-learner logistic regression to maximise generalised accuracy of model predictions. The model allows for contextual environmental data and specific object data (bounding box area, speed of object, and environmental data/conditions - temperature, humidity, conditions) as parameters from the traffic video clips. The model contributes to the performance of prediction across diverse traffic and environmental conditions by permitting multi-source data to merge.

Standard machine learning algorithms that include Linear Regression, Random Forest, KNN, Decision Trees, and SVR. Results of the study show clear evidence of favourable results from the use of the ensemble framework, demonstrated by the evaluations of RMSE, MAE, and R^2 scaling metrics. Scalable and Reproducible Architecture: Developed a model with a modular and flexible architecture that supports easy configuration and data reproducibility.

The model can now be expanded to additional datasets, other cities, and traffic monitoring implementations. The method demonstrates the ability to extract frames, detect objects using YOLOv8, and engineer features in video streams at near real-time, which could be deployed as video feeds for smart city surveillance and ITS systems. By having temporal, spatial, and contextual features as inputs, the model produces more realistic and context-based prediction outputs, given that real-world factors such as time of day, climate, and traffic component variables can change. This study demonstrates the framework for developing future intelligent traffic management systems with the predictive module that will be used for adaptive signal control, predictive alerts for congestion, and smart routing recommendations.

6.3 Public Relevance

The study of traffic congestion prediction using ensemble deep learning and video traffic measurements has important implications and applications. The rapid urbanization and increase in vehicle numbers within metropolitan areas have already resulted in severe levels of traffic congestion, impacting both daily commuting and economic productivity. Moreover, public transport systems often cannot anticipate or adjust to the variability in traffic patterns without traffic forecasting instruments.

This work presents an ensemble of deep learning models, CNN-LSTM, MLP, and SVC, which yields significantly better prediction accuracy for congestion levels than the individual use of the model algorithms. Additionally, the ensemble model utilizes real-time video feeds and identifies weather conditions, providing improved contextual understanding and situational awareness for traffic congestion forecasting.

The ensemble model allows traffic authorities to take proactive measures to respond to changing traffic conditions, adjust signal timing, and facilitate emergency vehicles. Traffic congestion has high costs as it relates to pollutant emissions and fuel consumption. With less idle time in traffic and driving time potentially reduced as traffic controls are implemented, these costs can be reduced as well. Overall, this research provides a meaningful contribution to the process of developing intelligent transportation systems spanning scale, operational efficiency, and meets the characterised needs of smart city development.

The research on traffic congestion prediction using ensemble deep learning and video traffic data has far-reaching implications and applications. With rapid urbanization and increasing vehicles, public transportation in metro cities often struggles with adequately regulating traffic movement. The design of intelligent traffic management systems is critical to fostering improved urban mobility, decreased pollution, and increased commuter safety and convenience. An ensemble deep learning model has the following relevance in the public transportation system

- Improving real-time traffic management
- Improving road safety
- Reducing environmental footprint
- Supporting smart city developments

- Reducing economic losses caused by traffic delays
- Reducing accidents by forecasting congestion hotspots

6.4 Challenges Faced

Obtaining traffic data of high quality and of sufficient variety proved a significant challenge due to the need for up-to-date traffic flow, road weather conditions, and videos with annotations for the analysis. In some situations, the missing or not fully compatible data impacted the quality and readability. Processing large-scale video data for object detection using deep learning models, especially the ensembling method, consumes a lot of computational power. Furthermore, the temporal conditions on lighting, occlusions, and changes to the scene affected the performance of YOLOv8.

The models achieved using deep learning methods, and especially the ensemble method, required a lot of computational resources, and needed to be tuned for hyperparameter exploration for all base learners (e.g., CNN-LSTM, MLP, SVC), and tuning each of the base learners took time and multiple iterations to arrive at a final learner. Being able to ensure that the model could smartly process the associated data and make predictions in real-time proved difficult; however, the real-world applicability and ability to make accurate predictions in real-time proved to be worth it. Merging and aligning different types of data (i.e., traffic flow, road weather conditions, visual aspects of object detection) required complex alignment of the data, and included data extraction and pre-processing steps that slowed down the overall development.

6.5 Future Work

While the findings from this work are promising, a reasonable next step could be focusing future work on model deployment into a real-time traffic management application to provide real-time congestion notification and route recommendations. Test, develop, and adapt the model for different urban settings and traffic patterns in different cities to develop robustness to generalised performance. Merging video data with other traffic datasets (i.e., GPS, loop detectors, and IoT devices) can provide a holistic picture of road conditions. More Advanced Meta-Learning - Future work can compare the predictive power of more advanced meta-learning models (i.e., Gradient Boosting Machines or Neural Networks) in ensemble stacking.

As video surveillance technology is more generically used to analyse traffic patterns, future work should also address ethical and privacy-preservation measures involving the sourcing and processing of such data. Future work could ultimately integrate other forms of anomaly detection techniques to uncover anomalous traffic events (i.e., accidents, road blockages, or vehicle malfunctions) that could assist with emergency responders' actions and reduce congestion. Another major opportunity for future work could be working to enhance the interpretability of the ensemble model using SHAP values or LIME, which would aid traffic authorities in explaining what features are leading to congestion and would also afford more transparency to decision-making.

www.ingramcontent.com/pod-product-compliance
Lightning Source LLC
LaVergne TN
LVHW010728061126
851857LV00014B/1386